Ninjaz Foody Digital Air Fry Oven Cookbook

Easy And Delicious Recipes With Your Foody Air Fryer Oven

BY KENZIE WRIGHT

Table of Contents

indirect, which are incurred as a result of the use of information contained within this document, including, but not limited to, — errors, omissions, or inaccuracies.

INTRODUCTION

An air fryer is a kitchen machine that cooks by flowing hot air around the food utilizing the convection instrument. It is a scaled-down adaptation of the convection oven. A mechanical fan circles the hot air around the menu at a fast rate, cooking the food and delivering a fresh layer using browning responses of two sorts. In caramelization, sugars separate and artificially change into complex dark-colored shaded substances, while in the Maillard response, ordinarily observed where meat is cooked or pan-seared, the starches/sugars and proteins in a food respond with one another to frame Schiff bases, which at that point structure other tasty mixes, including darker ring compound containing at least one nitrogen molecules in the ring, for example, pyrazines and pyridines. The Maillard response requires temperatures of between 280-330°F (140-165°C), while caramelization temperatures rely upon the sugar being caramelized and run from 230-360°F (110-180°C).

The Ninjaz foody is a weight cooker and air fryer that can likewise be utilized as an oven, steamer, roaster, dehydrator, and moderate cooker. Ninja's thought is to give you Tender Crisp foods from one apparatus. To accomplish this, the Ninja has two tops: a separable weight cooking cover for delicacy and a non-removable crisping top. The Ninja turned out with the new Ninjaz foody Deluxe 8-quart. The new Foody Deluxe has another treated steel finish. They've switched up the UI to a utilization focus dial and colossal LCD screen. It additionally includes a bigger cooking limit and another yogurt button. The Ninjaz foody Pressure Cooker is easier to use. It works likewise to the Instant Pot and other electric weight cookers.

Customary searing techniques instigate the Maillard impact by totally submerging foods in hot oil, which accomplishes extensively higher temperatures than bubbling water. The air fryer works by covering the ideal food in a thin layer of oil while flowing air warmed up to 200 °C (392 °F) to apply warmth and start the response. By doing this, the apparatus can darken foods like potato chips, chicken, fish, steak, cheeseburgers, French fries, or cakes utilizing 70% to 80% less oil than a conventional profound fryer.

Most air fryers have temperature and clock changes that permit increasingly exact cooking. Food is prepared in a cooking bin that sits on a dribble plate. The container and its substance must be occasionally shaken to guarantee even oil inclusion. Top of the line models achieves this by joining a food instigator that ceaselessly shakes the food during the cooking procedure. Though, most air fryers require the client to play out the undertaking physically at occasional interims. Convection ovens and air fryers are comparative in the manner they cook food, however air fryers are commonly littler in limit than convection ovens and emit less warmth.

The taste and consistency of foods cooked by conventional seared and air singed methods are not indistinguishable, because the more significant amount of oil utilized in conventional broiling infiltrates the foods (or the covering hitter, if it is used) and includes its very own flavor. Correctly, if food is covered distinctly in a wet hitter without an outside obstruction of a dry covering like breadcrumbs that are squeezed solidly to guarantee grip, the air fryer's fan can blow the player (or free scraps) off the food. Some air fryers are outfitted with embellishments, for example, pizza containers, stick racks, and cake barrels.

CHAPTER ONE

WHAT IS THE NINJAZ FOODY DIGITAL AIR FRY OVEN AND HOW IT WORKS

Second, just to the Instant pot, air fryers are as yet one of the most sizzling kitchen contraptions available. Be that as it may, these creations, which regularly fill only one need, gobble up a lot of significant counter space. No big surprise, there's been a rash of new items that try to consolidate air fry innovation with the conventional appliances individuals as of now have in their kitchens.

The most recent entry, the Ninjaz foody Digital Air Fry Oven, works off the accomplishment of the current Ninjaz foody items by consolidating an air fryer and toaster oven into one helpful bundle. However, is it worth the venture? The Ninjaz foody oven could combine two bits of gear in one without relinquishing on the presentation of either.

The functionality of the Ninjaz foody Digital Air Fry Oven works

When you remove it from the crate, you get a feeling that the Foody Digital Air Fry Oven is a unique item. Developed of brushed tempered steel, it's delightfully completed with adjusted corners and has a digital control cushion. It's likewise more extensive and shorter than a regular toaster oven. When cooled and not being used, the Foody oven can be flipped up on one side to stand up at the rear of the counter, an odd, however advantageous stockpiling arrangement. As opposed to a towel bar handle in the front, it was a little irregular to the side that you use to open the entryway. While it's surprising and requires some investment to become acclimated to, this handles capacities superbly fine and helps make the oven more space effective.

The Foody Digital Air Fry Oven accompanies an air fry bushel, a cooking rack, a nonstick sheet skillet, and a morsel plate that additionally appears to be healthy and all around made. They're more significant than the ones you regularly find in a toaster oven, as the stove is so vast.

What the Ninjaz foody Digital Air Fry Oven does

As the name infers the Ninja oven air fries. What's more, much the same as an average toaster oven, this Ninja toasts, and heats? It additionally air cooks, air sears, gets dried out and keeps food warm. Since it's so short, nevertheless, it can't hold an entire chicken like many toaster ovens in its value class.

The maker supports utilizing the large sheet skillet to make sheet container meals and incorporates an equation and a few recipes for them. In case you're searching for other multi-useful appliances that can slow cook, pressure cook, flame broil, and that's just the beginning, Ninja likewise offers the exemplary Ninjaz foody Pressure Cooker, which we love, and the Ninjaz foody Grill, which we'll be trying this fall.

What we like

It's flawlessly planned.

The digital controls are anything but difficult to pursue and natural to explore.

It's tranquil.

It's a brilliant toaster and works admirably of baking a sheet container supper.

To check food, there's an oven light.

For capacity, it effectively can remain on its side.

What we don't care for

It's costly.

It can't cook an entire chicken.

There could be more cooking rules for explicit foods in the cookbook.

How can it perform?

Air Frying

To be obtuse, it's not the best air fryer available, but instead, it's likewise a long way from the most noticeably terrible. The Ninjaz foody oven air fries unevenly, and the food arranged without any preparation appeared to be heated, not seared. On the site, the producer claims it can air fry four pounds of food without a moment's delay. While we could accumulate that measure of chips in the air fry bin, the stacked bushel couldn't fit in the oven at the rack position suggested for air fricasseeing.

Toasting

The Foody Digital Air Fry Oven can oblige nine cuts of bundled bread without squishing them. What's more, it can toast them fairly equitably, as well. At the point when used to toast two cuts, it gives impressive outcomes, cooking incredibly equally. It does, in any case, toast to a brilliant dark colored shade on both the light and medium settings, so it could be a failure if you like your toast just softly cooked. It has a different bagel toasting setting, and it tans bagel parts consistently.

Air Roasting

Ninja prescribes utilizing their oven to air broil sheet dish meals with a protein (like steak, chicken, or seafood), vegetables and flavors. In the wake of following the oven booklet's recipe for Spicy Chicken, Sweet Potatoes, and Broccoli, you will be dazzled with the outcome. The entirety of the ingredients (around three pounds altogether) turned out delicately sautéed and delicate in only 22 minutes and made a delectable sheet skillet supper for four. This procedure seems like a generally excellent use for this apparatus.

Baking

You're not going to have the option to fit a whole portion or Bundt skillet in this Ninja, yet you can utilize it to prepare a cake or biscuits in a shallow container, or little things like treats directly on the sheet dish. Rolls heated up similarly just as from a full-size oven.

Air Broiling

Chicken bosoms turned out delicious and seared on the two sides in only 20 minutes. But, in any event, when cooked well-done, steaks looked dark outwardly and not the slightest bit took after seared or flame-broiled meat. Along these lines, while this oven is quick, it can't reliably convey the sort of burning you anticipate from broiling.

Dehydrating

Even though its full air fry bin holds more food than the ones in the regular air fryer (or the racks in a toaster oven), the Ninja is still just ready to dry a limited quantity of food. In the wake of running the dehydrator for 10 hours, I was rewarded with a little bowl of banana chips. At any rate, the machine stayed silent as it worked.

Keep Warm

The Ninja kept a little macaroni and cheese dish at a sheltered serving temperature for an entire two hours. As you would expect, in any case, the food was dried out at that point. In case you're not going to serve food within a half-hour or thereabouts, you are likely happier, only warming it in the microwave.

The Ninjaz foody Digital Air Fry Oven simple to utilize and clean

The digital control board on the Ninja oven is all around spread out and simple to peruse. It interfaces bases on a handle that you go to choose the time and temperature (or several cuts and doneness) for each capacity, and it's relatively intuitive to program.

The way that the oven preheats consequently and the preheat time is only one moment, so it doesn't add obviously to the cooking time. During cooking, the item is calmer than most air fryers, and you can turn on an inside light to keep an eye on your food's advancement. The sheet container and the air fry bushel can be cleaned in the dishwasher. The standing position, the back opens, giving you access to within for cleaning.

The Ninjaz foody oven accompanies a thorough and straightforward proprietor's guide, just as a booklet that contains recipes and cooking graphs for air browning and drying out and a handout with instructions on the most proficient method to assemble a sheet dish meal. It would be useful if there were likewise diagrams to use as rules for baking, air roasting, and air-broiling.

The Foody Digital Air Fry Oven was just being sold through Ninja's site, where it had 64 audits and a star rating of 4.9. It's presently additionally accessible at Amazon, Walmart, and different retailers. In their remarks, its initial adopters rave about its multi-usefulness, huge limit, and speed. They likewise love the capacity to flip it up and stand it up and off the beaten path when it's not being utilized.

The Ninjaz foody Digital Air Fry Oven - Is It Worth the Price?

In case you're searching for an air fryer and a toaster oven, this item is undoubtedly worth your thought. It's a fantastic toaster and good air fryer. The main genuine downsides are that it has an enormous impression on your ledge and can't cook an entire chicken. And, if you have the counter space and are prone to purchase rotisserie chickens at the general store, we state to pull out all the stops.

The across the board kitchen wizard that may supplant different appliances.

Stroll into any hardware or excellent home store, and you'll discover no deficiency of kitchen appliances professing to be different things in one. However, they seldom work out. The electric can opener with the wine stopper remover never fills in just like the devoted apparatus, and I'm humiliated by how often I've succumbed to this. My kitchen isn't especially huge, so space is including some hidden costs, which is hard for somebody who wants to investigate better approaches to cook.

With the world being decidedly invaded by multipurpose weight cookers at present, Ninja got my attention with its new Foody cook framework. Over contribution a full weight cooker, it's likewise an air fryer? It sounded unrealistic, and however, after a little extra research, it immediately turned out to be clear this is a real multipurpose cooking framework worth a spot in my kitchen.

Ninja is offering a perfect quality weight cooker and a not too lousy air fryer in a similar contraption, with incredibly basic instructions for changing from one cooking mode to the next. For those anxious to spare some space in the kitchen, this is the best approach.

Pros

• Simple to utilize

• Easy to clean pieces

• No deficiency of extras

• Consistently conveys a similar encounter

Cons

• No approach to store pieces you aren't utilizing

• No auto modes for straightforward cooks

The notoriety of pressure cookers nowadays makes me too cheerful, and realizing this has happened because advanced innovation has made them more secure is fantastic. I love how a cutting edge pressure cooker will pop an alert at you when something is consuming on the base of the pot, or the weight isn't being kept up. PCs have taken weight cookers and made them microwave straightforward with regards to things like eggs or steaming veggies. The distinction in flavor or how quickly you can cook has a significant effect on families on a tight timetable or spending plan.

The pressure cooker mode on the Ninjaz foody is like the others you'll discover available today. Supplement a pot in the bigger cooking vessel, fill it with the stuff you need to cook, and afterward utilize the front board to set temperature and prepare time. It's a dead-straightforward framework, however, route more secure to use than pressure cookers of old. Simply adhere to the instructions, search for an enjoyment recipe, and start testing. You can pick between the standard 6.5-quart pot model or the more significant (and increasingly costly) 8-quart model for more celebrated families. Also, not at all, like most other electronic weight cookers, the two models accompany an artistically covered pot as opposed to making you pay extra for it. The fired covering makes it substantially simpler to clean, as most foods don't adhere to that surface as effectively as it does harden steel or aluminum.

As an independent electric pressure cooker, the Ninjaz foody is incredible. It could without much of a stretch consolidate a pressure cooker and a moderate cooker into a solitary contraption for most people and be incredible by and extensive experience. Nonetheless, if you evacuate the fired pot and snatch the other top, you'll discover in the crate, this cooker will likewise function as an air fryer. By adding a fan framework to the warming component, Ninja can cause it so you can drop in an air fryer crate and cook everything from solidified food to whole chickens. Since the air fryer tech doesn't depend on bubbling oil to cook, the subsequent menus are commonly viewed as more sound than the other options. That doesn't mean you can't include a little oil for a season or even put some meat over the highest point of veggies, so the drippings fall and douse into different things you're cooking. It's another degree of control in the kitchen, and again by and large, more secure to use than a conventional oil fryer.

It merits bringing up Ninja hosts been amazingly cordial to third gatherings in making embellishments for the Foody as of now, which is incredible. A speedy hunt uncovered outsider steam diverter, silicone slings to effortlessly move hot spots around the kitchen, and even cake skillet so you can heat legitimately in this cooker. Ninja itself makes a lot of different frills also, including a stick stand, and extra airflow represents less customary cooking strategies. In that short assortment, I found out about at any rate three different approaches to cook with this thing that I generally never would have even tried to consider. By being so amicable toward other frill creators, Ninjas has guaranteed a dynamic network of home cooks will share a wide range of recipes only for this thing. What's more, trust me, they do.

Effectively my preferred thing about the whole experience Ninja is making here is the straightforwardness with which you can clean the entire thing. The earthenware covered pot, for when you're pressured or slow cooking, can be hurled directly in the dishwasher. Also, the air fryer mode is straightforward to clear out when you're done utilizing it. The two covers remembered for the bundle are likewise easy to clean, which is fundamental when in case you're similar to me and attempt to make numerous meals seven days in a weight cooker and don't have a huge amount of time. I can make a whole intricate meal in this one machine and have negligible tidy up when I'm set. That by itself makes it advantageous to me.

Ninjaz foody: Is this for you? I think so

There are a huge amount of electronic pressure cookers available today, some with way more name acknowledgment than others. In any case, what makes any of these the best thing for you is how you're going to utilize it, and that incorporates recurrence? In case you're an easygoing home cook and are getting a charge out of curiosity, you might be energized by value more than highlights. In case you're not very positive about your capacities as a home cook, you may favor comfort over things like crude force or a huge amount of highlights.

Ninja's Foody cooker has shown the capacity to do a lot of things quite well, which is fairly extraordinary in this space. By including a utilitarian air fryer in a manner that can work as an independent gadget when you have it set up that way, this turns out to be more about space-sparing and cleaning comfort than all else. Air fryers can be incredibly helpful when they're ground-breaking enough to cook huge things, and this is that. What's more, in case you're battling to discover space on your counters for numerous quality devices, having the option to unite into a solitary machine is amazingly significant.

What You'll Love

• The Original Ninjaz foody is very much made and solid.

• The Foody has an exceptionally decent showcase window that mentions to you what's happening in the pot, how much time is left, and indications to close the top.

• Blue lights on the showcase turn in a square while the Foody is pressurizing, and they quit pivoting when it has arrived at pressure.

• The manual included with the Foody was useful and simple to follow.

• A cookbook is incorporated just as a cooking cheat sheet for generally cooked things

• A Cook and Crisp bin and a reversible rack that works in high and low positions are incorporated.

• The nonstick clay covering on the pot appears to be very much made (some favor earthenware to hardened steel).

• The air fryer works superbly of crisping up foods.

• The air fryer time tallies down and stops after the time is up, so you don't need to remain in the space to stop it.

• The pot is somewhat shorter and more extensive than the Instant Pot (I accept, so you get increasingly surface territory for better searing), so you can undoubtedly fit four custard cups in the pot without stacking them over one another. Extraordinary for sweets, (for example, creme Brule) or for making singular parts, (for example, egg biscuits).

What You Need to Know Before Buying

• The Ninjaz foody Tender Crisp Pressure Cooker is a major and substantial machine, so you'll have to get a major space accessible to utilize it.

• The crisping top (air fryer top) is pivoted and not removable. You need space for the crisping cover to be open while utilizing the weight cooking top. The joined air fryer cover implies you can't cook with the Foody on a counter under your cupboards.

• The Foody electrical rope is just 33 crawls long, so it should be near an outlet to utilize it. (The instructions state not to utilize an electrical string.)

- The pressure discharge valve on the Foody is short and somewhat more troublesome than the Instant Pot to move without carrying your skin into contact with the steam.

- Hot air returns out from the of the unit as its air searing, so you'll have to put it away from dividers and cupboards.

- Many frills that fit in most 6-quart pressure cookers will be too tall to even think about using in the Foody.

- The blare toward the end, when your time is up, isn't exceptionally uproarious and not customizable.

What You'll Love about the Ninja Deluxe

The Ninjaz foody Deluxe offers all the incredible capacities remembered for the first Ninjaz foody, and The Ninjaz foody Deluxe additionally has the accompanying new highlights

New Finish and Dial

The tempered steel outside is pretty and looks increasingly smooth and complex. The upgraded UI highlights a huge focus dial that makes setting the time and temperature simpler.

Bigger Cooking Capacity

The bigger 8-quart cooking pot accompanies a 5-quart Cook and Crisp container. It allows you to cook for a greater gathering. The 8-qt. The Cooking pot is nonstick and simple to hand-wash. The

5-quart Cook and Crisp bushel is clay covered, dishwasher safe, and holds as much as a 7-pound chicken.

You can find in the image underneath how much greater the Deluxe crate is contrasted with the one that accompanied the first 6.5-quart Ninjaz foody.

New Yogurt Function

Ninja added a yogurt capacity to the Ninjaz foody Deluxe. (My Instant Pot Yogurt recipe will function admirably in the Foody Deluxe.)

Other Great Features

The two-piece rack is reversible and stackable so you can oblige more food when steaming, broiling, or air browning.

The top is simpler to adjust because of the white line on the lodging and the weight cooking cover. This encourages you all the more effectively set up the pressure cooking cover.

The Ninja Deluxe Pressure Cooker has a dark fixing ring, which encourages it to stand apart from other weight cooker rings. (This is particularly helpful on the off chance that you have more than one brand.)

The blaring sounds are stronger on the new Deluxe.

What You'll Need to Know Before Buying

It's Still Heavy

The Ninjaz foody Deluxe is still very substantial, tipping the scales at 26 pounds. Since the crisping cover still isn't removable, you'll need to lift that weight each time you move or clean it. The non-removable top additionally makes it hard to fit under organizers.

No Progress Bar

The greater LCD screen is decent. It says [Pre] when the pressure cooker is coming to pressure, which is extraordinary, so you comprehend what's happening in the pot.

However, it has three sections of glimmering lights that don't compare to the advancement coming to pressure. I would have favored an advancement bar like a portion of the new electric weight cookers have.

Time Counts in Minutes and Seconds

Something else to know about when pressure cooking, the presentation includes down in minutes and seconds, not hours and minutes like the Instant Pot and numerous other weight cookers.

Instant Pot versus Ninjaz foody

On-screen cooking masters make everything look nauseatingly simple. Rather than storing a different ledge apparatus for each unique cooking technique you may require, these multifaceted gadgets handle capacities from sautéing to broiling, to cooking a pot cook 2-10 times quicker than a customary moderate cooker.

That is the reason gadgets like the Instant Pot have gotten blazingly well-known lately. (Also, why contenders like the Ninjaz foody are quick on their heels.)

Is the Ninjaz foody an Instant Pot?

In a word — no. Yet additionally, kind.

Instant Pots have been accepting much-merited recognition since the principal model turned out in 2008. Individuals fixated on it so much that it felt like no machine could ever even share the spotlight. However, Ninja, a fairly sudden contender that was centered on very good quality blenders, found a route in. The Ninjaz foody is likewise a pressure cooker and does a lot of what the Instant Pot got popular for, in addition to one other significant thing that the Instant Pot can't do: air fricasseeing.

This contention is working up some genuine dramatization. The "Instant Pot versus Ninjaz foody" banter is the focal point of incalculable articles, Reddit strings, and YouTube surveys. You can scarcely scan for one without Google auto-filling the other one.

Which is better: Ninjaz foody versus the Instant Pot

Regardless of whether the Instant Pot or Ninjaz foody is better isn't a no holds barred fight. Both have LCD screens, various weight settings, embeds that are dishwasher safe, and the remainder of those normal specs. But, the expression, "it's what's within that matters," has never been so precise (truly), and which cooker you ought to get relies upon the apparatus includes that you'll use on an increasingly normal premise. Continue perusing as we jump further into where every gadget wins and loses.

Where Instant Pot wins: More models with progressively customized highlights

"Instant Pot" is an umbrella term. Like a grandma hollering "or whatever your name is" to a gaggle of grandkids, the Instant Pot family is adaptable to the point that it tends to be difficult to recollect which model does which — however that is something worth being thankful for.

There are at present ten gadgets in the IP lineup: the most essential being the 6-in-1 Lux for $59.95 and the most vigorous being the 11-in-1 Max for $199.95. Each Instant Pot can pressure cook, slow cook, cook rice, steam, sauté, and warm, and as the models level up, progressively modern highlights are included, similar to yogurt making or sous vide.

Most models are accessible in the famous 6-quart size just as a little 3-quart model and a family-accommodating 8-quart model.

(There is no 3-quart rendition of the Foody.) Instant Pot models shift so broadly to where they're practically adjustable to your ability and spending plan. Costs for the Foody start at $199.99 and maximize at an incredible $279.99, the main distinction between the two models being the size. It's a very little elbow room if you ask us.

However, where the Instant Pot truly hits home is how simple it makes recipes that are customarily an agony. Rice never ends up directly on the stove, yet the Instant Pot has nailed that saturated however not very clingy surface. A hurried breakfast is less upsetting when you can hard-bubble, delicate bubble, or poach an egg without contemplating it. Gracious, you neglected to remove the chicken from the cooler once more? You can even now defrost it and have a force separated garlic cook inside the hour. Best of all, if you needn't bother with those capacities, Instant Pot won't make you pay for them

However, more liquidized recipes like soups plunge and stews are by all accounts the Instant Pot's area of the expert. Each model has worked in brilliant projects that get more explicit than the number of appliances it replaces: bean/bean stew, meat/stew, soup/juices, sauté, poultry, steam, congee, multigrain, rice, pressure cook, warm, and moderate cook. Purées require an uncommon tender loving care, particularly when meat is cooking at the same time in the dish. These projects are now pre-set with the time and temperature required for that particular surface, disposing of a great part of the mystery on your end. It truly opens up your choices for meal prep and more advantageous eating — this tech journalist from Business Insider didn't accept the publicity about pressure cookers until he encountered the Instant Pot Ultra.

The Instant Pot Max additionally stands apart with 15 PSI, which makes for considerably quicker pressure cooking (the Foody comes to around 12 PSI). Wannabe gourmet specialists, grandmothers, and homesteaders will especially welcome the 15 PSI for its pressure canning capacities.

Where Instant Pot loses

Nobody truly minded that the Instant Pot couldn't air fry until the Foody tagged along. Presently, in spite of the Instant Pot having the option to do a ton of things that the Foody can't, it's a central factor for individuals who were attempting to settle on a pressure cooker an air fryer. Instant Pot released its air fryer, the Instant Vortex Plus, yet it comes up short on the entirety of the other Instant Pot highlights in this manner, still expects you to purchase two gadgets.

No air fricasseeing implies no crisping top — and that implies that the singed, darkened taste isn't possible in the Instant Pot. Rather, you'll need to remove your food from the Instant Pot and stick it in the oven to sear, while the Foody completes your meal without driving you to air freight the food somewhere else (and chance dropping it on the floor.)

Fewer clusters will be fundamental in the littler Foody also. Instant Pot's moderate size is a 6-quart while the Foody's sister size is a 6.5-quart. That additional half-quart could be immaterial for your needs. However, different commentators who have the two gadgets state that they saw the distinction.

Where Ninjaz foody wins: Air browning and crisping are difficult to leave behind

Air fryers were the blessing to give during the 2018 Christmas season. Air searing and pressure cooking are two of the most sizzling patterns in easygoing cooking at this moment, and Ninja having them both in a similar gadget implies some entirely substantial mounted guns. Since air searing is an oil-less (it requires a tablespoon or less) option in contrast to splashing food in a tank of oil, the Foody is likewise a pretty extraordinary buy for anybody on a fat-confined eating regimen.

At the core of the first Foody is Ninja's Tender Crisp innovation. The thing superbly crisps the skin of the chicken or scorches veggies, a method that you could already just truly get with a grill or conventional oven. (Ok, with the goal that's the reason it's known as the weight cooker that crisps.) Both the 6.5-quart and XL 8-quart models can likewise heat, sear, sauté, steam, slow cook, and dry out, and the XL can make yogurt.

A few people lean toward that fresh surface on everything. The Instant Pot can knead huge cuts of meat similarly just as the Foody, however, the Foody tans and squeezes up skin such that other ledge appliances haven't generally had the option to accomplish. The comfort of accomplishing that through the basic switch of a top on the Foody is tremendous, particularly for individuals who take their brittle chicken wings and pork skins as truly as Guy Fieri.

What's more, on account of the tall flame broil rack, the Foody can cook veggies, grains, and meat simultaneously. So can the Instant Pot, however, the Foody has increasingly surface zone on the base, hence giving more space to lay your food down a level for all the more, in any event, cooking without flipping.

Where Ninjaz foody loses

Who's that Pokémon? Even though the Foody and the Instant Pot are comparative in the limit, the Foody is cumbersome, strangely formed, and resembles it's wearing protective layer. What's more, talking about feelings, just the 8-quart model comes in tempered steel (though all Instant Pots get that treatment). The more reasonable 6.5-quart model is dim dark and looks shabbier. Both are truly overwhelming and not perfect for lifting on and off the counter.

Adding to the ponderousness is the cover circumstance. The Tender Crisp-ing must be finished with an alternate, bigger top, which is joined to the Foody using pivots and disrupts the general flow when you're just utilizing the weight cooking top. You'll require at any rate 21 crawls of room to flip the crisping cover-up, so on the off chance that you have cupboards over your counter, this could demonstrate testing. It is alluded to the twofold cover structure as "humorously enormous."

The ninja doesn't offer such a large number of choices with regards to "modifying" your cooker to your needs. While you can purchase an Instant Pot for $50 on the off chance that you just need six machine capacities, purchasing a Foody secures you in spending, in any event, $199. What's more, it's a bummer that the Foody is so expensive and doesn't have a treated steel embed. It's not as delicate as Teflon, yet there are reports of chipping from the metal rack being pulled in and out. A few people likewise aren't happy with their food chilling in a plastic-y fired covering for a considerable length of time.

The verdict: It's a toss-up

When settling on your buy choice, simply recollect that the two gadgets do things that the other one can't. Exchanging up how you cook meat is the Foody's wheelhouse, and those air fryer and crisping capacities are a selling point that can't be disregarded. Then again, Instant Pot removes the mystery from touchy dishes like soups, plunges, and rice, and offers progressively one of a kind highlights like cake making, pressure canning, and sous vide. However, if you won't utilize that enormous cluster of capacities, there are increasingly essential Instant Pot models that will cost you substantially less. If Instant Pot discharges a weight cooker that can air fry, poop will go down.

CHAPTER TWO

NINJAZ FOODY AIR FRY OVEN RECIPES – BREAKFAST AND BRUNCH

Easy Air Fryer Omelet

This Easy Air Fryer Omelet is prepared in a short time, so there unquestionably aren't any reasons for skipping breakfast. When you prep your omelet ingredients, you can either do it in the first part of the day or shakers them up the prior night. I will be, in general, shakers them up the prior night. At times I cut up more than what I need, so I have enough veggies for two mornings worth of omelets.

For a two-egg omelet, for instance, I would hack up around 1/4 cup of new mushrooms and two tablespoons (or something like that) every one of the remainders of the ingredients.

Ingredients

- 2 eggs

- 1/4 cup milk

- Pinch of salt

- Fresh meat and veggies, diced (I utilized red chime pepper, green onions, ham, and mushrooms)

- 1 teaspoon McCormick Good Morning Breakfast Seasoning – Garden Herb

- 1/4 cup destroyed cheese (I utilized cheddar and mozzarella)

Instructions

- In a little bowl, blend the eggs and milk until all around consolidated.

- Add a touch of salt to the egg blend.

- Add your veggies to the egg blend.

- Pour the egg blend into a well-lubed 6″x3″ dish.

- Place the dish into the bushel of the air fryer.

- Cook at 350º Fahrenheit for 8-10 minutes.

- Halfway through preparing sprinkles, the breakfast flavoring onto the eggs and sprinkle the cheese over the top.

- Use a slight spatula to slacken the omelet from the sides of the dish and move to a plate.

- Garnish with additional green onions, discretionary

Air Fryer Bacon

Ingredients

• 6 portions of bacon

Instructions

- Place the bacon in the base of your air fryer crate. I have a 3.5-quart air fryer and had the option to get 6 portions of bacon on the base. Spot the wire rack over your bacon that accompanied the air fryer. This is discretionary. On the off chance that you don't have a wire rack that accompanied your air fryer, at that point, you needn't bother with one.

- Cook for 350 for 7 to 9 minutes. Open up the air fryer and flip the bacon. Put the air fryer crate back in and cook for an additional 3 minutes or until anyway fresh you like your bacon.

Quick Air Fryer Breakfast Pockets

Ingredients

- one box puff cake sheets

- 5 eggs

- 1/2 cup hotdog disintegrates, cooked

- 1/2 cup bacon, cooked

- 1/2 cup cheddar cheese, destroyed

Instructions

- Cook eggs as standard fried eggs. Add meat to the egg blend while you cook, whenever wanted.

- Spread out puff baked good sheets on a removing board and cut square shapes with a cutout or blade, ensuring they are on the whole uniform so they will fit pleasantly together.

- Spoon favored egg, meat, and cheese combos onto half of the baked good square shapes.

- Place a baked good square shape over the blend and press edges together with a fork to seal.

- Spray with shower oil on the off chance that you wanted a gleaming, smooth cake, yet it truly is discretionary.

- Place breakfast pockets in the air fryer bin and cook for 8-10 minutes at 370 degrees.

- Watch cautiously and check every 2-3 minutes for wanted done-ness.

Air Fryer Baked Apple

Your preferred oat or natively constructed apple granola on the planet couldn't beat this incredibly hot, shamefully tasty Air Fryer Baked Apple.

This recipe turns crude, healthy ingredients into something unrecognizable in an ideal manner conceivable. Air fryers are a blessing from above making sugary, caramelized, and mellowed treats feasible, regardless of what your weight reduction objective.

All you need is only a smidge of spread and cinnamon. This Baked Apple (or pear!) recipe is an American most loved sure to bring solace your way without busting the calorie bank. Indeed, Air Fryer Baked Apples check in at less than 150 calories (with starches of the SmartCarb assortment), however, bring the bread kitchen taste of a portion of your preferred calorie-loaded baked goods. Presently how would you like dem apples? Bend over for a flex nibble.

While one Extra is noted per serving, you'll see that this recipe is additional everything in the flavor division.

Servings: 2

Calories per Serving: 139

On Nutrisystem, Count As 1/2 SmartCarb, 1/2 PowerFuel, and 1 Extra

Ingredients:

- 1 medium apple or pear

- 2 Tbsp. hacked pecans

- 2 Tbsp. raisins

- 1 ½ tsp. Light margarine, dissolved

- ¼ tsp. Cinnamon

- ¼ tsp. nutmeg

- ¼ cup of water

Directions:

- Preheat air fryer to 350° F.

- Cut the apple or pear down the middle around the center and spoon out a portion of the tissue.

- Place the apple or pear in a skillet (which might be furnished with the air fryer) or on the base of the air fryer (in the wake of expelling the frill).

- In a little bowl, consolidate margarine, cinnamon, nutmeg, pecans, and raisins.

- Spoon this blend into the focuses of the apple/pear parts.

- Pour water into the dish.

- Bake for 20 minutes.

Air Fryer Cinnamon Rolls

These sweet little cinnamon rolls prepare in only 10 minutes and have a grocery store alternate way by utilizing locally acquired bread batter as the base. If you need to make the batter without any preparation, that is fine as well!

Ingredients

- 1 pound solidified bread mixture, defrosted

- ¼ cup margarine, dissolved and cooled

- ¾ cup darker sugar

- 1½ tablespoons ground cinnamon, Cream Cheese Glaze

- 4 ounces cream cheese, relaxed

- 2 tablespoons margarine, mollified

- 1¼ cups powdered sugar

- ½ teaspoon vanilla

Instructions

- Let the bread mixture come to room temperature on the counter. On a delicately floured surface, fold the batter into a 13-inch by 11-inch square shape. Position the square shape, so the 13-inch side is confronting you. Brush the dissolved margarine everywhere throughout the mixture, leaving a 1-inch outskirt revealed along the edge most remote away from you.

- Combine the dark-colored sugar and cinnamon in a little bowl. Sprinkle the blend equitably over the buttered batter, keeping the 1-inch outskirt revealed. Fold the mixture into a log beginning with the edge nearest to you. Roll the mixture firmly, making a point to move uniformly and push out any air pockets. At the point when you find a workable pace edge of the mixture, press the batter onto the move to seal it together.

- Cut the sign into eight pieces, cutting gradually with a sawing movement, so you don't straighten the mixture. Turn the cuts on their sides and spread with a spotless kitchen towel. Let the moves sit in the hottest piece of your kitchen for 1½ to 2 hours to rise.

- To make the coating, place the cream cheese and spread in a microwave-safe bowl. Mellow the blend in the microwave for 30 seconds one after another until it is anything but difficult to mix. Bit by bit includes the powdered sugar and mix to join. Include the vanilla concentrate and race until smooth. Put in a safe spot.

- When the rolls have risen, pre-heat the air fryer to 350°F.

- Transfer 4 of the moves to the air fryer craze. Air-fry for 5 minutes. Turn the turns over and air-fry for an additional 4 minutes. Rehash with the staying four rolls.

- Let the moves cool for two or three minutes before coating. Spread enormous bits of cream cheese coat over the warm cinnamon rolls, enabling a portion of the coating to dribble down the side of the rolls. Serve warm and appreciate it!

Gluten-Free Cranberry Pecan Muffins Air Fryer Recipe
A Quick and Easy gluten-free Cranberry Pecan Muffin recipe for a Holiday Brunch, or a flavorful biscuit any time of the year. Cranberries are in many heated things throughout the fall and winter months. We make cranberry sauce for Thanksgiving and proceed through Christmas with a lot more recipes to which we include cranberries.

We don't need to confine baking with cranberries just to fall and winter months. Treats and biscuits with new cranberries can be for whenever of the year. You can generally get a solidified sack of cranberries when crisp cranberries are out of season.

To be straightforward, I've just utilized new cranberries a couple of times as of recently. I've bounced into the cranberry lowland this year and made a few biscuits and a speedy bread with crisp cranberries.

Truly, they were compelling. The cranberries heated consummately, including a flavorful poignancy. If you have to loosen up toward the evening, make some tea and appreciate this gluten-free cranberry walnut biscuits air fryer recipe.

Biscuits are tasty for breakfast whenever of the year. This being a blender recipe causes this a recipe you too can prepare right away by any means. So how about we get baking!

Ingredients

- 1/4 cup cashew milk (or utilize any dairy or non-dairy milk you like)

- 2 huge eggs

- 1/2 tsp. vanilla concentrate

- 1 1/2 cups Almond Flour

- 1/4 cup Monk fruit (or utilize your favored sugar)

- 1 tsp. baking powder

- 1/4 tsp. cinnamon

- 1/8 tsp. salt

- 1/2 cup new cranberries

- 1/4 cup cleaved walnuts

Instructions

- Add to blender container the milk, eggs, and vanilla concentrate and mix 20-30 seconds.

- Add in the almond flour, cinnamon, sugar, baking powder,

- and salt – mix another 30-45 seconds until very much mixed.

- Removed the blender container from the base and mix in the 1/2 of the crisp cranberries and the walnuts. Add the blend to silicone biscuit cups. Top every one of the biscuits with the rest of the new cranberries.

- Place the biscuits into the air fryer crate and prepare on 325 for 12-15 minutes – or until toothpick confesses all.

- Remove it from air fryer and then cool on wire rack.

- Drizzle with a maple coat whenever wanted. You can additionally showered softened white chocolate over a portion of the biscuits.

Air Fryer Homemade Strawberry Pop-Tarts

Air Fryer Homemade Strawberry Pop-Tarts is a speedy and simple sound recipe with refined without sugar icing utilizing diminished fat cream cheese, vanilla Greek yogurt, and stevia. An amicable child recipe that is incredible for grown-ups, as well! Air Fryer Homemade Strawberry Pop-Tarts might be my best creation yet! I am certain the greater part of you recollect Pop-Tarts. Some of you may, in any case, eat Pop-Tarts, or feed them to your youngsters. I have exceptionally affectionate recollections from my youth that include Pop-Tarts. For reasons unknown, my mother, as often as possible, obtained the seasoned cinnamon kind. I don't have anything against cinnamon. However, the strawberry season tasted better to a youngster!

Ingredients

- 2 refrigerated pie coverings I utilized Pillsbury

- 1 tsp cornstarch

- 1/3 cup low-sugar strawberry jam I utilized Smucker's

- 1/2 cup plain, and non-fat vanilla Greek yogurt

- 1 oz diminished fat Philadelphia cream cheese

- 1 tsp sugar

- 1 tsp stevia

- Olive oil and coconut oil shower

Instructions

- Lay the pie outside layer on a level working surface. I utilized a bamboo cutting board.

- Using a blade or pizza shaper, cut the 2 pie outside layers into 6 square shapes (3 from every pie covering). Each ought to be fairly long as you will overlay it over to close the pop tart.

- Add the jam and cornstarch to a bowl and blend well.

- Add a tablespoon of the jam to the outside layer. Spot the jelly in the upper territory of the outside layer.

- Fold each of them over to close the pop tarts.

- Using a fork, make engraves in every one of the pop tarts to make vertical and even lines along the edges.

- Place in the Air Fryer. Splash with oil. I like to utilize olive oil.

- Cook on 375 degrees for 10 minutes. You might need to monitor the Pop-Tarts around 8 minutes to guarantee they aren't unreasonably fresh for your enjoyment.

- Combine the cream cheese, Greek yogurt, and stevia in a bowl to make the icing.

- Allow the Pop-Tarts to cool before expelling them from the Air Fryer. This is significant. If you don't enable them to cool, they may break.

- Remove the pop-tarts from the Air Fryer. Top each with the icing. Sprinkle sugar sprinkles all through.

Blueberry Lemon Muffins Air Fryer Recipe

Blueberry Lemon Muffin Air Fryer Recipe a simple to make biscuit for breakfast or brunch, Mother's Day, Father's Day. The biscuits can likewise be oven heated at 350 degrees for 12-15 minutes.

Ingredients

- 2 1/2 cups self-rising flour

- 1/2 cup Monk Fruit (or utilize your favored sugar)

- 1/2 cup cream

- 1/4 cup avocado oil

- 2 eggs

- 1 cup of blueberries

- zest from 1 lemon

- juice from 1 lemon

- 1 tsp. of vanilla

- brown sugar for fixing (a bit of sprinkling over every biscuit, not exactly a teaspoon)

Instructions

- In a little bowl, combine oneself with rising flour and sugar. Put in a safe spot.

- In a medium bowl, consolidate cream, oil, lemon juice, eggs, and vanilla.

- Add the flour blend to the fluid blend and mix just until mixed. Mix in the blueberries.

- Spoon the hitter into silicone cupcake holders, sprinkle ½ tsp — darker sugar over every biscuit.

- Bake at 310 degrees for 11 minutes. Check biscuits at 6 minutes to guarantee they are not cooking excessively quickly. Put a toothpick into the focal point of the biscuit, and when the toothpick tells the truth and the biscuits have caramelized, they are finished. No compelling reason to over-prepare the biscuits, they will keep on cooking for one more moment or two after they are expelled from the air fryer.

- Remove and cool.

Air Fryer Frittata

Air fryers make for a consummately light approach to appreciate the entirety of the flavor of your seared, oily top picks in a thinned down manner, and this Air Fryer Frittata is a prime (pardon the joke) "eggs-abundant."

Rather than staring off into space about the "eternity taboo" brunch foods the entirety of your companions are getting a charge out of, make a light, protein-pressed and delicious meal that will dispatch your day in the correct direction. Mushrooms, tomato, and chive draw out the serious weapons for the crisp garden flavor to supplement cushy billows of egg white that needs no help from cheese.

The Air Fryer Frittata is presumably the best value for your PowerFuel money that you'll have throughout the day at only 75 calories. Our preferred thing about this frittata is how adaptable it is. Appreciate half as is, and you have an ideal bite. In any case, if it's a full breakfast, you're after, top half with your preferred low-fat cheese, and serve it with a side of new natural product, and you have yourself an awesome flex breakfast.

Ingredients:

- 1 cup egg whites
- 2 Tbsp. skim milk

- ¼ cup cut tomato

- ¼ cup cut mushrooms

- 2 Tbsp. slashed new chives

- Black pepper, to taste

Directions:

- Preheat Air Fryer at 320° F.

- In a bowl, join every one of the ingredients.

- Transfer to a lubed griddle (which might be furnished with the air fryer) or to the base of the air fryer (in the wake of expelling the adornment)

- Bake for 15 minutes or until frittata is cooked through.

Air Fryer: Breakfast Puffed Egg Tarts

The Air Fryer Breakfast Puffed Egg Tarts are made with heavenly destroyed cheese, puff cake, and eggs. Straightforwardness reigns in these rich, yet at the same time simple, egg tarts. Puff cake concocts and around each egg, framing an ideal home.

Tips to Make Egg Tarts

The sheet of puff cake ought to be around 9 inches (23 cm) square for this recipe. If your sheets are an alternate size, or the baked good arrives in a square, fold or trim it into a 9-inch (23 cm) square as vital. Air fryers become exceptionally hot, particularly when warmed to most extreme temperatures. Use oven cushions or gloves when contacting the machine and when opening and shutting the container.

To make including the egg simpler, break the egg into a little cup before sliding it onto the puff baked good. Makes four tarts

Ingredients

- All-reason flour
- 1 sheet solidified puff baked good a large portion of a 17.3-oz/490 g bundle, defrosted
- 3/4 cup destroyed cheese, for example, Gruyere, Cheddar or Monterey Jack, separated
- 4 enormous eggs
- 1 tbsp minced crisp parsley or chives discretionary

Instructions

- On a gently floured surface, unfurl cake sheet. Cut into 4 squares.
- Place 2 squares in the air fryer bin, dividing them separated. Air-fry for 10 minutes or until baked good is light brilliant dark-colored.
- Open bin and, utilizing a metal spoon, push down the focuses of each square to make a space. Sprinkle 3 tbsp (45

mL) cheese into every space and cautiously break an egg into the focal point of every baked good.

- Air-fry for about 11 minutes or until eggs is cooked to wanted doneness. Move to a wire rack set over waxed paper and let cool for 5 minutes. Sprinkle with a large portion of the parsley, whenever wanted. Serve warm.

- Repeat steps 2 to 4 with the rest of the cake squares, cheese, eggs, and parsley.

Recipe Notes

The sheet of puff cake ought to be around 9 inches (23 cm) square for this recipe. On the off chance that your sheets are an alternate size, or the cake arrives in a square, fold or trim it into a 9-inch (23 cm) square as vital. Air fryers become extremely hot, particularly when warmed to the greatest temperature. Use oven cushions or gloves when contacting the machine and when opening and shutting the container. To make including the egg simpler, break the egg into a little cup before sliding it onto the puff cake.

Air Fryer Heavenly French Toast

This is one of the most effortless breakfast recipes, that is found in French Toast. The player is rich and makes a pleasant and light hitter, that when I joined it with air broiling, it turned out decent and fleecy.

Ingredients

- 4 cups of bread

- 2 eggs

- ⅔ cup of milk

- 1 teaspoon of vanilla

- 1 tablespoon of cinnamon

Instructions

- In a little bowl, combine the eggs, milk, cinnamon, and vanilla. At that point, beat until the eggs are separated, and everything is blended well.

- Then plunge each bit of bread into the blend and afterward shake to get the abundance off, as you do, put them into your readied container

- Air Fryer for 4 minutes at 320 degrees F. At that point, flip them over and do an additional 3 minutes.

- Serve with maple syrup and appreciate it!

Guilt-free Paleo Pumpkin Muffins in The Air Fryer

This recipe is stunning because it utilizes a great deal of the rudiments of pumpkin pie filling alongside some additional chocolate produce to give you the ideal biscuit. It has common sugar in it, so it's ideal for sugar longings and gratitude to the way that you needn't bother with that much pumpkin to make it is fairly efficient.

Ingredients

- 1 Cup Pumpkin Puree
- 2 Cups Gluten-Free Oats
- ½ Cup Honey
- 2 Medium Eggs beat
- 1 Tsp Coconut Butter
- 1 Tbsp Cocoa Nibs
- 1 Tbsp Vanilla Essence
- 1 Tsp Nutmeg

Instructions

- Place every one of your ingredients in the blender and mix until smooth.
- Place the biscuit blend into little biscuit cases, spreading it out more than 12 separate ones.
- Place in the Air Fryer and cook for 15 minutes on 180c.
- Serve when cool.

Notes

you can make it all the more chocolatey by including some cocoa powder and some wrecked bits of dull chocolate, yet I favor it like the recipe above.

Hash Brown Recipe

This hash dark-colored recipe is nearly oil-free, you can utilize only a little brush of oil for this air fryer recipe. Figure out how to make simple breakfast hash tans and joy your children. This is a sound option in contrast to the general skillet variety of a dark-colored hash recipe. This hash darker recipe is nearly oil-free, you can utilize only a little brush of oil for this air fryer recipe. Figure out how to make simple breakfast hash tans and pleasure your children.

Ingredients

- Large potatoes - 4 - stripped and finely ground
- Corn flour - 2 tablespoon
- Salt - to taste
- Pepper powder - to taste
- Chili pieces - 2 teaspoon
- Garlic powder - 1 teaspoon (discretionary)
- Onion Powder - 1 teaspoon (discretionary)

- Vegetable Oil - 1 + 1 teaspoon

Instructions

- Soak the destroyed potatoes in cool water. Channel the water. Rehash the step to empty abundance starch of potatoes.

- In a non-stick container, heat, 1 teaspoon of vegetable oil and sauté destroyed potatoes till cooked marginally for 3-4 mins.

- Cool it down and move the potatoes to a plate.

- Add corn flour, salt, pepper, garlic, and onion powder and bean stew drops and combine generally.

- Spread over the plate and pat it solidly with your fingers.

- Refrigerate it for 20 minutes

- Preheat air fryer at 180C

- Take out the now refrigerated potato and partition into equivalent pieces with a blade

- Brush the wire container of the air fryer with little oil

- Place the hash dark colored pieces in the crate and fry for 15 minutes at 180C

- Take out the bushel and flip the hash tans at 6 minutes with the goal that they are air singed consistently

- Serve it hot with ketchup

Air-Fried Cinnamon and Sugar Doughnuts

This adaptation utilizes an air fryer. By utilizing less oil, I can utilize more delicious oil. In this manner, my decision is spread. Serve and eat hot. Like conventional doughnuts, they are greatly improved hot than cold.

Ingredients

- 1/2 cup white sugar

- 2 1/2 tablespoons spread, at room temperature

- 2 huge egg yolks

- 2 1/4 cups generally useful flour

- 1 1/2 teaspoons baking powder

- 1 teaspoon salt

- 1/2 cup acrid cream

- 1/3 cup white sugar

- 1 teaspoon cinnamon

- 2 tablespoons spread, softened, or varying

Instructions

- Press 1/2 cup white sugar and spread together in a bowl until brittle. Include egg yolks and mix until very much consolidated.

- Sift flour, baking powder, and salt into a different bowl. Spot 1/3 of the flour blend and 1/2 the acrid cream into the sugar-egg blend; mix until joined. Blend in the rest of the flour and sharp cream. Refrigerate mixture until prepared to utilize.

- Mix 1/3 cup sugar and cinnamon in a bowl.

- Roll mixture out onto a delicately floured work surface to 1/2-inch thick. Cut 9 enormous circles in the batter; cut a little hover out of the focal point of every huge hover to make donut shapes.

- Preheat the air fryer to about 350 degrees F (175 degrees C).

- Brush 1/2 of the liquefied spread over the two sides of the doughnuts.

- Place 1/2 doughnuts into the container of the air fryer; cook for 8 minutes. Paint cooked doughnuts with the staying softened spread and quickly dunk into the cinnamon-sugar blend. Rehash with the rest of the doughnuts.

Air Fryer Breakfast Toad-in-the-Hole Tarts

Ham, egg, and cheese settled inside a fresh and feathery tart. These little jewels are sufficiently amazing to serve to visitors, yet straightforward enough to make quickly.

Ingredients

- 1 sheet solidified puff baked good, defrosted

- 4 tablespoons destroyed Cheddar cheese

- 4 tablespoons diced cooked ham

- 4 eggs

- chopped crisp chives (discretionary)

Directions

- Preheat the air fryer to about 400 degrees F (200 degrees C).

- Unfold well baking sheet on a level surface and cut into 4 squares.

- Place 2 baked good squares in the air fryer bushel and cook 6 to 8 minutes.

- Remove bin from the air fryer. Utilize a metal tablespoon to press each square tenderly to shape space. Spot 1 tablespoon of Cheddar cheese and 1 tablespoon ham in each gap and pour 1 egg over each.

- Return bushel to air fryer. Cook to wanted doneness, around 6 minutes more. Expel tarts from the container and let cool 5 minutes. Rehash with residual cake squares, cheese, ham, and eggs.

- Garnish tarts with chives.

Easy Air Fryer French Toast Sticks

These simple-to-make French toast sticks end up extraordinary in an air fryer. The dry your bread out first, so you don't wind up having your bread self-destruct during the dousing procedure. Present with your preferred French toast fixings, for example, powdered sugar, sugar and cinnamon blend, or syrup.

Ingredients

- 4 cuts marginally stale thick bread, for example, Texas toast

- material paper

- 2 eggs, delicately beaten

- 1/4 cup milk

- 1 teaspoon vanilla concentrate

- 1 teaspoon cinnamon

- 1 squeeze ground nutmeg (discretionary)

Instructions

- Cut each cut of bread into thirds to make sticks. Cut a bit of material paper to fit the base of the air fryer bushel.

- Preheat air fryer to about 350 degrees F (180 degrees C).

- Stir together eggs, milk, vanilla concentrate, cinnamon, and nutmeg in a bowl until all around consolidated. Plunge each bit of bread into the egg blend, ensuring each piece is all around submerged. Shake each breadstick to evacuate overabundance fluid and spot in a solitary layer in the air fryer container. Cook in bunches, if fundamental, to abstain from congestion the fryer.

- Cook for about 5 minutes, and turn bread pieces and cook for an extra 5 minutes.

Air Fryer Sausage Patties

Air fry your wiener patties, and you will maintain a strategic distance from oil splatter all over your stovetop. The best part is, the patties will be pleasantly cooked

Ingredients

- 1 (12 ounces) bundle wiener patties

- 1 serving nonstick cooking splash

Instructions

- Preheat the air fryer to 400 degrees F (200 degrees C).

- Place wiener patties into the bin in 1 layer, working in clumps if essential.

- Cook in the preheated air fryer for 5 minutes. Haul the crate out, turn the meat over, and cook until an instant-read thermometer embedded into the focal point of a patty peruses 160 degrees F (70 degrees C), around 3 minutes more.

Easy Air Fryer Omelet

Arranged in the air fryer and loaded up with new veggies and cheese, this omelet is delicious and prepared in a short time!

Ingredients

- 2 eggs

- 1/4 cup milk

- Pinch of salt

- Fresh meat and veggies, diced (I utilized red chime pepper, green onions, ham, and mushrooms)

- 1 teaspoon McCormick Good Morning Breakfast Seasoning – Garden Herb

- 1/4 cup destroyed cheese (I utilized cheddar and mozzarella)

Instructions

- In a little bowl, blend the eggs and milk until very much consolidated.

- Add a spot of salt to the egg blend.

- Add your veggies to the egg blend.

- Pour the egg blend into a well-lubed 6″x3″ container.

- Place the container into the bushel of the air fryer.

- Cook at 350° Fahrenheit for 8-10 minutes.

- Halfway through preparing sprinkles, the breakfast flavoring onto the eggs and sprinkle the cheese over the top.

- Use a slender spatula to relax the omelet from the sides of the skillet and move to a plate.

- Garnish with additional green onions, discretionary

Air Fryer Breakfast Pizza

Searching for something straightforward, however, yet delicious for breakfast? Attempt my Air Fryer Breakfast Pizza recipe. This is such a simple put-together breakfast pizza that will prevail upon your children and life partner. A light and flaky covering, stacked with cheese, eggs, and can't overlook hotdog.

Ingredients

- Crescent Dough

- 3 fried eggs

- crumbled hotdog

- 1/2 hacked pepper

- 1/2 cup cheddar cheese

- 1/2 cup mozzarella cheese

Instructions

- Spray Pan with oil,

- Spread batter in the base of a Fat daddio or springform dish

- Place in the air fryer on 350 for 5 minutes or until the top is somewhat dark colored

- Remove from the air fryer

- Top with Eggs, sausage, peppers, and cheese or utilize your preferred garnishes.

- Place in the air fryer for an extra 5-10 minutes or until the top is brilliant dark-colored.

Notes

You can utilize any fixings you wish

Air-Fried Ham and Egg Toast Cups

Ingredients:

- 4 Ramekins (I purchased mine from Daiso at $2 each!)

- 4 Eggs

- 8 Slices of Toast (Preferably whole meal for an increasingly healthy breakfast)

- 2 Slices of Ham (I utilized Chicken Ham. However you can utilize whichever you like)

- Butter

- Salt

- Pepper

- Cheese (Optional)

Instructions

- Initially, brush the inside of the ramekin with a liberal measure of margarine with a cooking brush. The more margarine, the simpler it is to expel the toast cups from the ramekins.

- Straighten 8 cuts of toast with either a moving pin or your palm. Make it as level as could be expected under the circumstances

- The line within every ramekin with a cut of smoothed toast. I know it's somewhat odd to crush a square into a hover, and there's most likely bound to be abundance bread collapsing inwards. Be that as it may, attempt to squeeze the additional folds and make it as decent a cup as could reasonably be expected.

- Spot another cut of leveled toast over the principal toast and, in like manner, attempt to straighten the additional folds.

- Cut 2 cuts of ham into 8 littler strips.

- Line 2 pieces of ham in every ramekin. See picture above for reference

- Break an egg into each toast cup

- Include a touch of salt and some ground dark pepper into each egg

- You may likewise include some cheese into the toast cup (as observed previously). By and by, I utilized 1 cut of cheddar cheese and cut into little pieces.

- Spot every one of the 4 ramekins into the Air fryer for 15 mins at 160 degrees. You don't have to preheat the Air fryer ahead of time

- When done, expel the ramekins from the Air fryer with either a tea towel, silicone tongs, or whatever kitchen contraception you have that shields your fingers from the warmth.

- To expel the toast cup from the ramekins, I utilized a little blade and gradually cut it round within the ramekin just on the off chance that some bread stalled out to the sides. At that point, I wriggled the toast cup out of the ramekin with a similar little blade and a spoon.

Spanish Frittata with Potato and Chorizo
Ingredients

- To fit a little container or the Phillips Air Fryer skillet
- 3 kind sized unfenced eggs
- ½ chorizo wiener – cut
- 1 major potato – standard bubbled and cubed
- ½ cup solidified corn
- olive oil
- cleaved herbs of your decision – I utilized parsley
- ½ wheel of feta
- salt/pepper

Instruction

Pour a decent glug of olive oil in the container of the Air Fryer(or your skillet on the stove), and include the chorizo, corn and the potato. Set the Air Fryer on 180C and cook the frankfurter and potato until somewhat seared. Break the 3 eggs into a little bowl and beat with a fork. Season with salt and pepper. Pour eggs over the potato and frankfurter in the dish and top with crumbled feta and slashed parsley. Cook for an additional 5 minutes, check and, if necessary, cook for one more moment or something like that. At the point when cooked, turn out on a plate and present with stout tomato relish and some new rocket.

But if you are doing it on the stovetop and oven, preheat the oven to 180C and afterward cook the potato and meat in an oven-verification skillet on the stovetop. At the point when the potato has sautéed marginally, beat the eggs in a little blow away and pour the potato and hotdog. Top with feta and parsley and heat in the oven until the eggs are set.

Breakfast-style air fryer potatoes

Is your stovetop space maximized with veggie bacon and tofu scramble? No stresses! Cook the breakfast potatoes in the air fryer and free up a portion of that valuable stovetop land. Additionally, you get potatoes out of the arrangement! It's a success win.

Ingredients

- 2 medium estimated Russet potatoes ~13 ounces absolute or approximately 2 liberal cups, hacked in about one-inch pieces

- Few liberal spritz oil shower

- Pinch salt and pepper

- 1 little ringer pepper ~5 ounces or around 3/4 cup, cleaved medium

- 1 little onion ~4 ounces or about 3/4 cup, slashed medium

Instructions

- Put potatoes into the air fryer bin. Spritz with oil shower, shake spritz once more, and include a spot of salt.

- Set the air fryer to 390 degrees and ten minutes. Stop once to shake during cooking time.

- After the potatoes have cooked for ten minutes, including the ringer pepper and onions. Include another spritz of oil, and shake the container. Set the air fryer to 390 degrees and 16 minutes.

- During the most recent 5 minutes of cooking, keep an eye on the potatoes to ensure they aren't getting excessively dark-colored. Contingent upon the size of your potatoes, you may require marginally less or somewhat additional time. If necessary, add a couple of more minutes to the cooking time.

- Add salt to taste and serve.

Air fryer French Toast Sticks Recipe

Take French Toast to another, the fresh spot with this Air fryer French Toast Sticks recipe.

Ingredients

- 4 pieces bread (whatever sort and thickness wanted)

- 2 Tbsp spread (or margarine, mollified)

- 2 eggs (tenderly beaten)

- 1 squeeze salt

- 1 squeeze cinnamon

- 1 squeeze nutmeg

- 1 squeeze ground cloves

- 1 tsp icing sugar (as well as maple syrup for trimming and serving)

Instructions

- Preheat Air fryer to 180 Celsius.

- In a bowl, delicately beat together two eggs, a sprinkle of salt, a couple of substantial shakes of cinnamon, and little portions of both nutmeg and ground cloves.

- Butter the two sides of bread cuts and cut into strips.

- Dredge each strip in the egg blend and organize it in Air fryer (you should cook in two clusters).

- After 2 minutes of cooking, delay the Air fryer, take out the dish, ensuring you place the skillet on a warm, safe surface, and shower the bread with cooking splash.

- Once you have liberally covered the strips, flip and shower the subsequent side too.

- Return dish to the fryer and cook for 4 additional minutes, checking the following two or three minutes to guarantee they are cooking equally and not consuming.

- When the egg is cooked, and bread is brilliant, dark-colored, expel from Air fryer, and serve right away.

- To trimming and serve, sprinkle with icing sugar, top with whip cream, shower with maple syrup, or present with a little bowl of syrup for plunging.

Air fryer Beetroot Chips

Regardless of whether you despise Beet, attempt it!! You will cherish these Beetroot chips.

Ingredients

- 2 Medium Sized Beetroot

- 1/2 Tsp Oil

- Salt to taste

- Pepper Optional

Instructions

- Wash the Beetroot, strip the skin, and put the skin in a safe spot. Utilizing a mandoline slicer, cut them slender. Then again, if you don't have a slicer, cut them consistently slight with your blade.

- Use the skin to color your prop in the event that you need to or dump it into your food squander.

- Spread the beetroot cuts on the paper and spot another paper over it. Keep it aside for 10 minutes. This procedure will empower to assimilate any additional dampness on the beetroot diminishes.

- Toss the cut beetroot in oil and sprinkle the required salt on the beetroot.

- Preheat the Air fryer to 150 C for 4 minutes. Pull the container from the air fryer and spot the chips in them. Slide it back in the air fryer and fry for 15 minutes. Make a point to expel in the middle of after at regular intervals and give it a decent shake. When the chips are somewhat fresh on the external edges and delicate in the center, enable them to chill off for quite a while.

- Slide the crate with the chips back again and heat at 180 C for an additional 3 minutes. The chips will be truly fresh by and large and impeccable to much immediately.

- Season with Sea Salt and newly ground pepper on the off chance that you like or simply chomp it for what it's worth. We love it in any case.

Air Fryer Shishido Peppers – Keto Recipe

This Keto amicable recipe is a snappy, simple, tasty low carb tidbit for any social affair or even only a peaceful night plunk down with your darling and a glass of wine!

Ingredients

- 1 6 oz pack Shishido peppers

- salt and pepper to taste

- 1/2 tbsp avocado oil

- 1/3 cup Asiago Cheese, ground fine

- Limes

Instructions

- Rinse the peppers with water and pat dry with paper towels. Spot in the bowl and hurl with avocado oil, salt, and pepper. The spot in the air fryer and cook at 350 for 10 minutes. Watch cautiously. You need them to turn out rankled looking, however not consumed.

- Place Shishido peppers on serving platter. Sprinkle with a little lime squeezed and top with ground asiago cheese. Serve!

Notes

Around 7 peppers for each serving. Fat 4g, Net Carb 1g, Protein 3g

Sustenance data determined to utilize MyFitnessPal is given as an obligingness, however, will differ contingent upon the particular brands of ingredients you use. If it's not with too much trouble counsel with your PCP in regards to explicit wellbeing needs.

Air Fryer French Fries

Air fryer French fries are the ideal method to make fries at home, and my family cherishes these!

Ingredients

- 3 medium potatoes (I am utilizing chestnut)

- 1/4 teaspoon of garlic powder

- salt and pepper to taste

- 1 1/2 tablespoons oil of decision (I love utilizing avocado oil since it has a high smoke point. Coconut likewise functions admirably.)

Instructions

- Wash your potatoes, and pat them dry

- Slice the potatoes to the size fries you need, and attempt to be to some degree steady with the size to take into account in any event, cooking. (Note: bigger fries may require marginally more cook time.)

- Toss the fries with the oil, garlic, salt, and pepper. You can hurl them in a bowl, or hurl them in your air fryer bushel if you are lethargic like me!

- Cook on 400 in the air fryer for around 20 minutes (more for bigger, steak fries), and hurl them around two or multiple times during the cooking to help equally cook.

- Taste whether you need progressively salt and pepper.

- If you need to make them look extravagant, sprinkle some hacked new parsley on top.

Coconut Shrimp with Spicy Marmalade Sauce

Firm and crunchy outwardly, delicate within, this Coconut Shrimp is at least somewhat sound. Dunked in the Spicy Marmalade Sauce, this is a gathering in your mouth.

Contemplations on the Air Fryer:

- If you make a great deal of solidified food, this is ideal for the activity. It makes pieces, fries, onion rings crispier than an oven ever could. Simply make sure to shake the crate during the cooking procedure for baking.

- Easy to clean... overly simple to clean.

- Do not utilize flour; simply don't do it.

- Spray your food with a touch of cooking splash for extra fresh outcomes.

- I wish it was prettier because the cumbersome plan takes up a ton of counter space, and it's an undeniable irritation to discover a spot to store it on the off chance that you have a modest kitchen.

- The bin size is little, so if you have an enormous family, you should cook in bunches. This will take quite a while. Just saying'.

Ingredients

- 8 enormous shrimp shelled and deveined

- 8 ounces of coconut milk

- 1/2 cup destroyed improved coconut

- 1/2 cup panko bread

- 1/2 teaspoon cayenne pepper

- 1/4 teaspoon genuine salt

- 1/4 teaspoon crisp ground pepper

- 1/2 cup orange preserves

- 1 tablespoon nectar

- 1 teaspoon mustard

- 1/4 teaspoon hot sauce

Instructions

- Clean the shrimp and put it in a safe spot.

- In a little bowl, whisk the coconut milk and season with salt and pepper. Put in a safe spot. In a different little bowl, whisk together the coconut, panko, cayenne pepper, salt, and pepper.

- One at once, plunge the shrimp in the coconut milk, the panko, and afterward placed in the bin of the fryer. Rehash until all the shrimp are covered. Cook in the fryer for 22 minutes at 350 degrees or until the shrimp are cooked through.

- While the shrimp are cooking, whisk together the preserves, nectar, mustard, and hot sauce.

- Serve the shrimp with the sauce right away.

Air Fryer Baked Sweet Potato

Ingredients

- 3 sweet potatoes

- 1 tablespoon olive oil

- 1-2 teaspoons genuine salt

Instructions

- Wash your sweet potatoes and afterward make air openings with a fork in the potatoes.

- Sprinkle them with the olive oil and salt, at that point rub uniformly on the potatoes.

- Once the potatoes are covered, spot them into the crate for the Air Fryer and spot into the machine.

- Cook the potatoes at 392 degrees for 35-40 minutes or until fork delicate.

- Top with your top choices!

Air Fryer Pork Taquitos

Yield: 10 Servings

Flavorful pork or chicken taquitos that are only 8 Weight Watchers Smart Points.

Ingredients

- 3 cups cooked destroyed pork tenderloin or chicken
- 2 1/2 cups fat-free destroyed mozzarella
- 10 little flour tortillas
- 1 lime, squeezed
- Cooking shower

Instructions

- Preheat air fryer to 380 degrees.
- Sprinkle lime squeeze over pork and delicately blend around.
- Microwave 5 tortillas one after another with a moist paper towel over it for 10 seconds, to relax.
- Add 2 oz. of pork and 1/4 cup of cheese to a tortilla.
- Tightly and delicately move up the tortillas.
- Line tortillas on a lubed foil-lined container.

- Spray an even layer of cooking shower over tortillas.

- Air Fry for 10 minutes until tortillas are a brilliant shading, flipping part of the way through.

- 2 taquitos per serving.

- But on the off chance that you don't have an air fryer, they can likewise be heated in the oven for 7 - 10 minutes on 375 degrees.

Notes

- Recommend 2 taquitos per serving

- Add discretionary things like salsa or sharp cream to plunge!

- Serve with guacamole and make a light meal that everybody will cherish.

- Weight Watchers Smart Points determined to utilize the Weight Watchers recipe manufacturer.

Air Fryer Sriracha-Honey Chicken Wings
Ingredients

- 1-pound chicken wings, tips evacuated, and wings cut into individual drumettes and pads.

- 1/4 cup nectar

- 2 tablespoons sriracha sauce

- 1 1/2 tablespoons soy sauce

- 1 tablespoon margarine

- juice of 1/2 lime

- cilantro, chives, or scallions for decorating

Instructions

- Preheat to 360 degrees F. Add the chicken wings to the air fryer container, and cook for 30 minutes, turning the chicken about at regular intervals with tongs to ensure the wings are equitably caramelized.

- While the wings are cooking, add the sauce ingredients to a little sauce skillet and heat to the point of boiling for around 3 minutes.

- When the wings are cooked, hurl them in a bowl with the sauce until completely covered, sprinkle with the enhancement, and serve right away.

Fresh Air Fryer Tofu with Sticky Orange Sauce

The Air Fryer Tofu is a helped up variant of the exemplary Chinese café dish. Blocks of tofu are covered in a tasty sweet and tart vegetarian orange sauce. No oil is expected to make this simple Asian solid recipe.

Ingredients

- 1 pound extra-firm tofu, depleted and squeezed (or utilize super-firm tofu)

- 1 Tablespoon tamari

- 1 Tablespoon cornstarch, (or arrowroot powder)

For the sauce:

- 1 teaspoon orange pizzazz

- 1/3 cup squeezed orange

- 1/2 cup water

- 2 teaspoons cornstarch, (or arrowroot powder)

- 1/4 teaspoon squashed red pepper pieces

- 1 teaspoon crisp ginger, minced

- 1 teaspoon crisp garlic, minced

- 1 Tablespoon unadulterated maple syrup

Instructions

- Cut the tofu in solid shapes.

- Place the solid tofu shapes in a quart-size plastic stockpiling pack. Include the tamari and seal the sack. Shake the pack until all the tofu is covered with the tamari.

- Add the tablespoon of cornstarch to the pack. Shake again until the tofu is covered. Put the tofu aside to marinate for at any rate 15 minutes.

- Add all the sauce ingredients to a little bowl and blend in with a spoon. Put in a safe spot.

- Place the tofu inside the air fryer in a solitary layer. You will presumably need to do this in two clumps.

- Cook at 380 degrees for 11 minutes, shaking it following 5 minutes.

- After you're finished cooking the bunches of tofu, add everything to a skillet over medium-high warmth. Give the sauce a mix and pour it over the tofu. Mix the tofu and sauce until the sauce has thickened, and the tofu is warmed through.

- Serve promptly with rice and steamed vegetables, whenever wanted.

Notes

Remains can be concealed and refrigerated for 3 days.

Veggie lover Air Fryer Crumble with Blueberries and Apple

Ingredients

- 1 medium apple finely diced

- 1/2 cup solidified blueberries strawberries or peaches

- 1/4 cup in addition to 1 tablespoon dark colored rice flour

- 2 tablespoons sugar

- 1/2 teaspoon ground cinnamon

- 2 tablespoons nondairy spread

Instructions

- Preheat the air fryer to 345°F for 6 minutes. Consolidate the apple and solidified blueberries in an air fryer–safe baking container or ramekin.

- In a little bowl, consolidate the flour, sugar, cinnamon, and spread. Spoon the flour blend over the natural product. Sprinkle some additional flour over everything to cover any uncovered natural product — Cook at 350°F for 15 minutes.

CHAPTER THREE

NINJAZ FOODY AIR FRY RECIPES – APPETIZERS

Air Fryer Bang Fried Shrimp

Air Fryer Bang Panko Breaded Fried Shrimp is the best, speedy and simple, sound, air-seared seafood recipe with bread morsels, sweet bean stew, and Sriracha plunging sauce. You can even attempt solidified or flame-broiled shrimp! Hoping to cut the carbs, set up this dish with no breading.

Air Fryer Bang Shrimp Recipe Tips:

- Find the greatest shrimp/prawns that you can! Enormous shrimp is a significant success for this recipe.

- Bang blast shrimp is a recipe that incorporates fresh, singed shrimp that is normally hurled in a zesty, sweet bean stew sauce. Rather than hurling the shrimp in the sauce, I chose to make a different plunging sauce. This will guarantee the shrimp remains crunchy for whatever length of time that conceivable.

- I additionally included plain, non-fat Greek yogurt to the plunging sauce to substitute. Greek yogurt likewise gives an extra increase in protein.

- If you don't have panko breadcrumbs available, standard breadcrumbs will work fine and dandy.

Ingredients

- 1 pound crude shrimp stripped and deveined
- 1 egg white 3 tbsp
- 1/2 cup generally useful flour
- 3/4 cup panko bread pieces
- 1 tsp paprika
- Chicken Seasoning for taste
- salt and pepper to taste

- cooking splash

Blast Bang Sauce

- 1/3 cup plain, non-fat Greek yogurt

- 2 tbsp Sriracha

- 1/4 cup sweet bean stew sauce

Instructions

- Preheat Air Fryer to 400 degrees.

- Season the shrimp with the seasonings.

- Place the flour, egg whites, and panko bread morsels in three separate dishes.

- Create cooking stations. Plunge the shrimp in the flour, at that point the egg whites, and the panko bread morsels last.

- When plunging the shrimp in the egg whites, you don't have to submerge the shrimp. Do a light touch with the goal that a large portion of the flour remains on the shrimp. You need the egg white to hold fast to the panko scraps.

- Spray the shrimp with a cooking shower. Try not to shower legitimately on the shrimp. The panko will go flying. Keep a pleasant separation.

- Add the shrimp to the Air Fryer container. Cook for 4 minutes. Open the container and flip the shrimp to the opposite side — Cook for an extra 4 minutes or until fresh.

Blast Bang Sauce

• Combine the entirety of the ingredients in a little bowl. Blend completely to join.

Heated Zucchini Fries Recipe

Hold up until you discover the mystery behind making this Baked Zucchini Fries Recipe! Air Baking is such a great amount of superior to browning food in oil. This air prepared zucchini fries recipe is so acceptable, and there's NO uncommon gear required.

Ingredients

- 3 medium zucchini cut into sticks
- 2 enormous egg white
- 1/2 cup prepared bread morsels
- 2 tbsp ground Parmesan cheese
- cooking shower
- 1/4 tsp garlic powder
- salt and pepper to taste

Instructions

- Preheat oven to 425.

- Place the cooling rack inside a baking sheet and coat rack with a cooking splash; put in a safe spot.

- In a little bowl, then beaten egg whites and season with salt and pepper.

- In another bowl, place breadcrumbs, garlic powder, and cheese and blend well.

- Dip the zucchini sticks into eggs then into bread morsel and cheese blend, a couple at once.

- Place the breaded zucchini in a solitary layer onto the cooling rack and splash all the more cooking shower on top.

- Bake at 425 for around 15-20 minutes, or until brilliant dark-colored.

- Serve with Ranch or Marinara sauce for plunging.

Heated Coconut Chicken Tenders

Heated coconut chicken tenders were a piece of a recently posted recipe for a tropical serving of mixed greens with coconut chicken and pineapple vinaigrette. This crunchy, delightful chicken goes consummately with the fruity tropical plate of mixed greens. Nonetheless, it's incredibly presented with anything. Along these lines, I'm making this post explicitly for the star of that tropical serving of mixed greens, the coconut chicken.

Making fresh heated chicken is an extraordinary option in contrast to making seared chicken. It's crunchy and tasty like singed chicken. However, it has significantly less fat. Nonetheless, this sort of chicken just remains firm for around 20 minutes. When it gets appropriately put away in the cooler, the covering mollifies. The flavor is as yet incredible. It's simply not firm. That is something to remember while deciding the amount of this chicken you need to make.

Ingredients

- 2 enormous eggs

- 2 tsp. garlic powder

- 1 tsp. salt

- 1/2 tsp. ground dark pepper

- 3/4 cup panko bread scraps

- 3/4 cup destroyed improved coconut

- 1 pound chicken tenders around 8 tenders

- cooking shower

Instructions

- Preheat oven to 400 degrees F. Shower an enormous baking sheet with cooking splash.

- In a wide shallow dish, including the eggs, garlic powder, salt, and pepper. Speed until very much consolidated. In a second wide shallow dish, include the panko breadcrumbs and destroyed coconut. Mix to consolidate.

- Dip the chicken tenders in the egg blend, covering the two sides. Lift the chicken out of the egg and enable the abundance to trickle off. Spot the egg covered chicken into the coconut blend. Press the coconut blend into the chicken, guaranteeing that all sides are covered. Spot the coconut covered chicken on the readied baking sheet. Dispose of the abundance egg and coconut blend. Shower the highest points of the chicken tenders with cooking splash.

- Bake on the center oven rack for 12-14 minutes until the chicken is cooked through, and the covering is fresh and brilliant dark-colored.

Seared Mac and Cheese Balls

Ingredients

- 4 cups remaining Mac and Cheese

- 1.5 cups prepared breadcrumbs (I utilized Garlic and Herbs)

- 1 egg

- 1 Tbsp milk

- Vegetable oil for fricasseeing

Instructions

- After the remains have been in the ice chest in any event medium-term, shape them into meatball-sized balls (or little chomps) and set them in a baking sheet secured with material paper.

- Cover the baking sheet with plastic and take it to the cooler medium-term.

- The following day, make an egg wash by beating the egg and the milk with a whisk. Put the egg wash in a bowl and the breadcrumbs in another.

- Dip the Macintosh and cheese balls in the egg wash and then in the breadcrumbs.

- Once every one of the balls has been breaded, returned them in the cooler for in any event 1 hour before searing.

- To fry, set a little pot loaded up with vegetable oil on the stove. Warmth the oil over medium warmth until 350 degrees. (If you don't have a thermometer, simply put a match inside. At the point when the match lights, the oil is prepared!)

- Turn the warmth down to medium-low and fry 5 or 6 balls one after another until they start getting brilliant darker.

- Turn the warmth up to high and complete the process of searing until the ideal shading: brilliant darker. (Remember to turn the warmth down again to sear the remainder of the cluster!)

Serve the balls warm with some marinara or nectar mustard sauce.

Crispy Air Fryer Potato Skins Just in Time for The Big Game

Making snacks for the folks during the Big Game doesn't need to be distressing or over the top. More often than not, they simply need great football food. Cold beverages and delectable appetizers are constantly hit during any gathering. One of my most well-known go-to appetizers has consistently been oven heated potato skins. This year I chose to put my new air fryer under a magnifying glass and prepare a bunch from beginning to end in under a fraction of the time it takes in a regular oven.

Fresh Air Fryer Potato Skins Just in Time for The Big Game! If you love firm potato skins stacked with all the great stuff, you have gone to the ideal spot — cooking them in the air fryer slices your time down the middle. All the scrumptious garnishes make them a hit with the entire family!

Ingredients

- 5 - 10 little baking potatoes - Baked early
- ½ Cup destroyed cheddar cheese
- ½ Cup disintegrated bacon
- Thinly cut chives.
- Dean's Bacon Cheddar Dip

Instructions

- Bake potatoes in the air fryer as indicated by maker directions. Each brand is extraordinary
- Be sure to season the outside with a sprinkle of oil and your preferred flavors.
- Once the potatoes are done and cool enough to deal with, cut every one fifty-fifty.
- Scoop out the greater part of the tissue from within the potato. Make certain to leave a decent sum around the edges.
- Sprinkle every half with cheddar cheese, and bacon disintegrates.

- Place them in a solitary layer back in your air fryer. Cook for 5 - 7 minutes or until the cheese is dissolved.

- Transfer them to a plate and top with cool and smooth Dean's Dip.

Air fryer Parmesan Dill Fried Pickle Chips

These handcrafted pickle chips are simpler to make then you would think. They require just five basic ingredients and meet up in under 30 minutes. To begin, you will need to cut huge dill pickles into 1/4″ thick cuts and spot them on a layer of paper towels. Pat them dry so the breading will adhere to them pleasantly.

Air fryer Parmesan Dill Fried Pickle Chips are a fast and simple five fixings hors d'oeuvre made extra crunchy in your Air fryer without all the fat from oil. This low-fat tidbit makes certain to fulfill your desire for something salty!

Ingredients

- 32 oz. container entire enormous dill pickles

- 2 eggs

- 2/3 c. panko bread morsels

- 1/3 c. ground Parmesan

- 1/4 tsp. dried dill weed

Instructions

- Slice the enormous pickles corner to corner into 1/4" thick cuts. The spot between layers of paper towels and pat dry.

- In a shallow bowl, beat the eggs until smooth. In a resealable sack, include the Panko bread morsels, Parmesan, and dill weed and shake until all-around joined.

- In bunches of 4-5 pieces, plunge the pickle cuts into the egg blend, being certain to expel any abundance egg and afterward hurl in the Panko blend.

- Add a portion of the covered pickle chips into the Air fryer and prepare for 8-10 minutes on the most noteworthy temperature. Expel from the Air fryer and include the rest of the pickle chips and prepare for 8-10 minutes. Serve promptly with the lively farm for plunging.

NOTE: If you have a bigger XL Air fryer, you can cook every one of the chips in a single bunch.

Air Fried Vegetable Spring Rolls

Brilliant and fresh vegetable stuffed spring rolls, cooked with insignificant oil inside an air fryer for a more beneficial, lighter treat

Ingredients

- 10 spring move sheets (see alternatives above)

- 1/4 yellow chime pepper, meagerly cut

- 1/4 red chime pepper, meagerly cut

- 5-6 mushrooms, cut

- 1 clove garlic, crushed

- 1 tsp galangal/ginger, minced

- 1 green onion, finely hacked

- 1/2 cup carrot, daintily cut

- 1/2 cup cabbage, daintily cut

- 2 feathered creatures eye chilies, finely slashed

- 1 tbs soya sauce

- 1 tbs vegetarian shellfish sauce (discretionary)

To serve

- 2 tbs sweet stew sauce

- 2 tbs soya sauce

Instructions

- In a little pot, sauté the green onion, ginger, and garlic until delicate and fragrant.

- Mix in the carrot, and following a couple of moments the remainder of the vegetables (aside from the chilies). The dish may appear stuffed; however, in no time flat, the vegetables will discharge their juices, and it will cook down perceptibly. Include the soy sauce and the shellfish sauce and cook for 10-12 minutes, blending periodically. When the container appears to be dry (no fluid is unmistakable when you move the vegetables around), remove the warmth, add the chilies to taste, and leave to cool totally.

- Remove the spring move sheets from the cooler and spread with fabric, for approx. Thirty minutes till the vegetables cool.

- Preheat the air fryer to 200 degrees.

- Place a solitary sheet on a perfect surface/plate in a precious stone shape (as presented previously). Spot a tablespoon full on the blend once inch from the triangle nearest to you. Roll most of the way firmly, fold on the left and right corners and keep rolling. It's quite simple.

- Place on the rack of the air fryer and brush with a tad of vegetable oil. Air fry, shaking at regular intervals and brushing with oil, if it looks dry. Your ideal brilliant dark-colored and overly fresh spring rolls will be prepared in less than 10 minutes.

- Enjoy presented with two plunging sauces - soy and sweet bean stew.

Notes

- I haven't taken a stab at freezing the stuffed spring rolls yet. I don't know whether the air fryer will respond well with solidified spring moves, as they will, in general, emit water while defrosting. Anybody attempted it yet?

- This blend of vegetables is discretionary. Use what you have at home.

- This measure of vegetable blend filled ten spring moves (which 2 of us ate up in a matter of seconds), so might need to twofold the recipe for wellbeing!

Coconut Shrimp with Piña Colada

Coconut Shrimp with Piña Colada is a solid, tropical summer starter. Air browning shaves off calories and fat, and my rendition is without gluten.

Ingredients

For the shrimp:

- 1 1/2 pounds kind sized shrimp

- 1/2 cup cornstarch

- 2/3 cup light coconut milk

- 2 tablespoons nectar

- 1 cup unsweetened destroyed coconut

- 3/4 cup panko bread scraps

For the sauce:

- 1/3 cup light coconut milk

- 1/3 cup plain nonfat Greek yogurt

- 1/4 cup pineapple lumps depleted

- 1/4 teaspoon salt more to taste

- 1/4 teaspoon pepper more to taste

- Toasted coconut for decorate

Instructions

- Remove the shrimp's shell , leaving the tail unblemished, whenever wanted.

- Place cornstarch in a gallon-size sack and include the shrimp. Hurl to cover.

- In a medium dish, whisk coconut milk and nectar until consolidated. In another medium bowl, consolidate coconut and panko. Expel shrimp from the pack, delicately knocking off any overabundance cornstarch. Dunk shrimp in the fluid blend. At that point, dig in the coconut blend.

You may need to press free coconut and panko tenderly onto the shrimp.

- Transfer covered shrimp to the bin of your air fryer. (I seared mine in two bunches since the covering is to some degree delicate.) Heat the fryer to 340 degrees F and cook 7-10 minutes, flipping shrimp once, until the coconut is brilliant darker and the shrimp are cooked through.

- Meanwhile, set up the sauce. In a medium bowl, join pineapple, salt, coconut milk, yogurt, and pepper in a dish.

Recipe Notes

To toast coconut, and preheat your oven or toaster oven to 400 degrees F. Set up a baking sheet with cooking splash. Spot coconut on the baking sheet in a solitary layer and heat for around 5 minutes until a portion of the coconut has turned a brilliant dark-colored.

Air Fryer Fried Wontons
Ingredients

You can also joke with the filling ingredients in these wontons from numerous points of view. You can utilize whatever kind of ground meat you like (I've utilized the entirety of the suggested meats on various events). Simply be cautious that you don't hold back on any of the ingredients that give genuine flavor, similar to the clam or sweet stew sauce, the soy sauce (see note underneath about sans soy ingredients), and the ginger and garlic.

Egg-free: You could have a go at making the wonton wrappers themselves with "chia eggs" (one "chia egg" is one tablespoon ground chia seeds + 1 tablespoon lukewarm water, blended and permitted to gel). However, there are three eggs in the recipe, so I'm not certain if it would work. What's more, the wrappers would be spotted with the seeds. Rather than egg wash to seal the edges of the wrappers, you can have a go at utilizing simple milk (nondairy milk if vital).

Soy-free: instead of conventional gluten-free soy sauce or tamari, you can utilize sans soy coconut amino; however, I do find that it has impressively less flavor than its soy-based cousin. I suggest multiplying the sum.

Air fryer free: See the recipe underneath for oven-baking and profound fryer directions!

Ingredients

- 1 recipe gluten-free wonton wrappers

- 1 pound ground chicken, hamburger, pork or white meat turkey

- 1 tablespoon finely ground new ginger (or 1/2 teaspoons ground ginger)

- 2 garlic cloves, stripped and finely ground or minced

- 2 tablespoons hacked scallions (from around 1 huge scallion, white and green parts)

- 1 tablespoon gluten-free soy sauce or tamari

- 2 tablespoons gluten-free sweet stew sauce (or 2 tablespoons gluten-free shellfish sauce)

- 2 cups hacked new greens, for example, kale, Brussels grows as well as cabbage

- Egg wash

- Oil, for covering (or for singing)

Directions

- Make the wonton wrappers as indicated by the recipe instructions, cut into around 3-inch squares. Put the wrappers in a safe spot. In an enormous bowl, place the meat, ginger, garlic, scallion, soy sauce, sweet bean stew sauce or clam sauce, and greens, and blend well to consolidate. The blend will be thick and moderately clingy.

- To collect the wontons, place a wonton wrapper level in the palm of your hand. Plunge the pointer of your free deliver the egg wash, and paint every one of the 4 edges of the wrapper with the egg wash. Include around 1 teaspoonful of the filling blend to the focal point of the wrapper. Overlap one corner of the wrapper catty-corner to the contrary corner to encase the filling. Seal the wrapper firmly around the filling, pressing out any air bubbles.

- Place the molded and filled wontons in the container of your air fryer in a solitary layer and shower or brush liberally with oil on the two sides. Spot in the air fryer and fry at 350°F for 4 minutes. Evacuate the container and shake it around, turning over whatever number of the wontons as could be expected under the circumstances. Return the bin to the air fryer and keep on searing for another 4 to 6 minutes, or until brilliant dark colored everywhere. Serve quickly with additional sweet stew sauce or soy sauce.

- **Alternate Oven-Baking Directions**: Prepare the wontons in a similar way; however, place them on a wire rack over the lined baking sheet around 1 inch separated from each other. Preheat your oven to 375°F. Utilizing a cake brush, cover the tops with an egg wash (1 egg beaten with 1 tablespoon water), at that point place in the focal point of the preheated oven and prepare for 12 minutes, or until softly brilliant dark-colored. They can likewise be bubbled in hot soup until delicate and cooked entirely through, around 5 minutes.

- **Alternate Deep-Frying Directions**: Similarly, prepare the wontons. Spot paper towels on a plate, and put it in a safe spot. Spot around 1/2 creeps of a neutral oil with a high smoke point (like nut or avocado oil) in a medium-size, overwhelming bottomed pan and carry the oil to 350°F over medium-high warmth. Add a couple of wontons to the oil to broil, sometimes turning until they are brilliant dark-colored, around 3 minutes. Expel them utilizing a filter to the paper-towel-lined plate to deplete. Take the oil back to the temperature between groups. Rehash with the rest of the wontons.

Air Fryer Mozzarella Sticks Recipe

These air fryer mozzarella sticks are a more beneficial interpretation of a most loved nibble exemplary! Skim string cheese sticks plunged in entire wheat flour, egg, panko breadcrumbs, and flavors: onion powder, garlic powder, salt, stew powder, and smoked paprika!

Ingredients

- 1 (10 oz) bundle part-skim mozzarella string cheese each stick cut down the middle

- 1/4 cup entire wheat flour

- 1 enormous egg

- 1/4 cup breadcrumbs

- 1/4 cup panko

- 1/2 - 1 teaspoon onion powder

- 1/2 - 1 teaspoon garlic powder

- 1/2 - 1 teaspoon salt

- 1/2 - 1 teaspoon bean stew powder

- 1/2 - 1 teaspoon smoked paprika

- Marinara sauce for plunging

- Ranch for plunging

Instructions

- Place divided cheese sticks into a Ziplock baggie and place in the cooler until solidified, in any event, 25 mins.

- Place the egg into a small bowl and race until separated. Put in a safe spot.

- Place breadcrumbs, garlic powder, panko, onion powder,

- salt, stew powder, and smoked paprika in another shallow bowl and speed until all-around joined. Put in a safe spot.

- Line rimmed baking sheet with a silicone tangle or material paper.

- Place solidified cheese sticks and flour into another Ziplock baggie (the one from the cooler will have too many ice lumps) and shake until the cheese sticks and completely covered in the flour.

- Discard overabundance flour.

- Dunk one cheese stick in egg until completely covered and afterward in panko blend until completely covered.

- Place on the fixed baking sheet and rehash with outstanding cheese sticks.

- Place the baking sheet in more refreshing until all the cheese sticks have re-solidified, in any event, 60 minutes.

- Hit "ON" broadcasting live fryer.

- Then hit "PRE-HEAT." Set the temperature to 360 degrees F and set the clock to 5 minutes.

- Hit "START."

- The air fryer will yell at you when it's done preheating.

- Open up the air fryer and splash the bin with a cooking shower.

- Place in the mozzarella sticks, work with around six at once, so you don't stuff them.

- Close the air fryer. It will blare at you when it's done cooking.

- Repeat with the same number of mozzarella sticks as you'd like. Store uncooked scraps in the cooler!

- Serve with plunging sauces and appreciate it!

Notes

Utilize one teaspoon every one of flavor on the off chance that you need an all the more forcefully prepared mozzarella stick!

Air Fryer Ravioli

Singed Ravioli is one of our preferred appetizers. This firm Air Fryer Ravioli is anything but difficult to make, yet extremely high. These are ideal for game day, parties, or even the family supper table.

Ingredients

For the Ravioli:

- 1 egg -, enormous

- 1/2 pack locally acquired smaller than regular cheese ravioli - (around 18-20 ravioli)

- non-stick canola cooking shower - (discretionary)

- 1 cup marinara sauce -, warmed, for plunging

For the Dredge:

- 1 cup Panko bread scraps

- 1/4 cup crisply ground Parmesan

- 1 teaspoon Italian flavoring

Discretionary Garnishes:

- 2 tablespoons Parmesan Cheese -, ground

- Instructions

- Set up a dig station with two dishes. In the first bowl, beat the egg. In the subsequent bowl, consolidate all the dig ingredients.

- Prepare the Ravioli. Keep the ravioli solidified until prepared to dig. Plunge the ravioli into the beaten egg. At that point, dig into breadcrumbs and put into fryer crate.

- Repeat. Rehash with residual ravioli.

- Cook the Ravioli: Spray the ravioli with a non-stick cooking splash (discretionary) to empower sautéing. Close the fryer crate and press power. Press the "M" symbol and select the "Fry" symbol. Increment the temperature to 400 degrees F. Set the opportunity to 12 minutes. Part of the way through, shake the container and turn the ravioli over. Include extra cooking shower, if necessary.

- Serve. Trimming with extra Parmesan cheese and serve hot with marinara sauce.

Air Fryer Frozen Onion Rings

Ingredients

- 1 pack Onion Rings solidified

- Instructions

- Place onion rings in the Air Fryer bin and set the temperature to 400 degrees Fahrenheit and set time for 8 minutes.

- Flip onion rings following 5 minutes.

Crisp lid Instructions

- Place trivet into the pressure cooker and spot a crisp lid bin on top.

- Place onion rings into a container and set the temperature to 400 degrees and set timer for 6 minutes.

- Flip onion rings following 4 minutes.

Notes

The brief cook time is only a proposal. A few people incline toward a gentler, less crunchy nibble. Start checking the onion rings at 5 minutes to check whether you might want to cook longer.

Air Fryer Buffalo Cauliflower
Cauliflower Wings – Variations

This recipe is a treat with bison sauce, yet that is only a glimpse of something more substantial with regards to making cauliflower wings in your air fryer!

you can utilize this strategy to make different kinds of air fryer cauliflower wings. Here are a few thoughts for you to attempt:

- teriyaki wings

- BBQ wings

- sriracha wings (or sriracha MAPLE wings — blend 2 tablespoons sriracha with 2 tablespoons maple syrup)

- jerk-prepared wings

Get innovative and make your delightful sauces. Since you merit a rainbow of cauliflower wings!

Ingredients

For the Cauliflower

- 4 cups cauliflower florets – Each one ought to be approx. The size of two infant carrots, on the off chance that you put the child carrots next to each other.

- 1 cup panko breadcrumbs blended in with 1 teaspoon ocean salt – I would not utilize common salt here. Ocean salt grains are higher, and they add some additional smash to the breading.

For the Buffalo Coating

- 1/4 cup liquefied vegetarian margarine – 1/4 cup in the wake of liquefying

- 1/4 cup veggie-lover Buffalo sauce – Check the ingredients for margarine. I utilized Frank's Red Hot

For Dipping

- vegan mayo – Cashew Ranch, or your preferred rich serving of mixed greens dressing

- Instructions

- Melt the vegetarian margarine in a mug in the microwave, at that point race in the wild ox sauce.

- Holding by the stem, plunge every floret in the margarine/wild ox sauce blend, getting the majority of the floret covered in sauce. It's okay if a touch of the stem doesn't get saucy. Hold the floret over the mug until it quits dribbling. A couple of trickles are OK, yet if it's coming down the sauce, your panko will get clumpy and stop staying also.

- Dredge the dunked floret in the panko/salt blend, covering as much as you can imagine, at that point, place in the air fryer. No compelling reason to stress over a solitary layer. Simply place it in there.

- Air fry at 350F (don't preheat) for 14-17 minutes, shaking a couple of times tenderly (see note), and checking their advancement when you swing. Your cauliflower is done when the florets are somewhat sautéed.

- Serve with your plunging sauce of decision.

Notes

- **About the Prep Time:** The 5-minute planning time expects that you purchased pre-cut, crisp cauliflower. In case you're utilizing an entire head, they will take longer. Solidified cauliflower won't work in this recipe.

- **About the Shaking**: You'll need to shake these delicately, particularly from the start. The player will get firmer as it cooks, yet if you stir too energetically, it will tumble off in the beginning times of cooking.

- **How to Reheat**: Buffalo cauliflower doesn't remain crunchy for long, so eat these promptly for most extreme goodness. You can warm these in the air fryer, so they'll get crunchy once more. I gave a portion of these to my neighbor during testing, and he cooked them in the oven with excellent outcomes, too. But if you warm in the microwave, they'll unquestionably be soft.

Air Fryer Chicken Wings

Air Fryer Chicken Wings are so fresh and tasty without utilizing any additional oil! Cooking Chicken Wings in an Air Fryer rather than profound broiling them makes them more advantageous and tidy up simpler. They are prepared in just 30 minutes, thus simple to make!

To what extent To Air Fry Chicken Wings

Chicken Wings take around 30 minutes in the Air Fryer, shaking the bin like clockwork, so the wings fresh up uniformly. Cooking the sides at a lower temperature first and afterward expanding the warmth throughout a previous couple of moments guarantees succulent wings with firm skin since this enables the fat to render out, so the skin gets extra fresh. This strategy brings about the BEST Chicken Wings!

Step by step instructions to Make A Bigger Batch

Fricasseeing the Wings in a solitary layer or isolated by a twofold layer rack works best. Yet, you can make a greater group by taking a portion of the wings out before expanding the temperature and crisping them up in little clusters. Simply try not to pack the bushel so the air can at the present circle. Watch the video beneath to perceive how I make a greater group in my littlest Air Fryer!

Would you be able to Cook Frozen Chicken Wings in An Air Fryer?

Indeed, you can cook solidified wings in an Air Fryer! On the off chance that you are utilizing solidified wings, air fry them 5 minutes longer at 380°F (29 minutes aggregate), before expanding the temperature throughout the previous 6 minutes to fresh them up. Try not to stress if the solidified wings remain together toward the start; simply make a point to shake the container following a couple of moments, so they get isolated.

Sauces and Seasonings for Wings

After air browning the wings, they get hurled with your preferred sauce or flavoring. That way, everybody can tweak their serving of wings. Below are a couple of our top choices:

- Buffalo Sauce: You can purchase this sauce or make your very own with only two ingredients (recipe in the recipe card)

- Garlic Parmesan Wing Sauce: Combine 1/4 cup softened spread, 1/4 cup ground Parmesan cheese, 1/2 tsp garlic powder, 1/4 tsp salt, 1/8 tsp ground dark pepper

- Honey Garlic Sauce

- Lemon Pepper

- Teriyaki Sauce: Salty and Sweet!

- Cajun Seasoning

- BBQ Sauce: Add as a lot of sauce as you like and hurl the wings!

- Old Bay Sauce: Melt 6 Tbsp unsalted margarine, include 2 tsp old inlet flavoring, and 2 tsp lemon juice. Hurl wings in sauce and residue with increasingly old inlet flavoring.

What to Serve with Chicken Wings?

Serve chicken wings (particularly those hurled in Buffalo Sauce) with Blue Cheese or Ranch plunging sauce and new celery and child carrots as an afterthought. Chicken wings are an exemplary canapé that additionally works out in a good way for coleslaw, fries, onion rings, chips, and seared mozzarella sticks. Ideal for a game day party!

Ingredients

• 2 lbs. chicken wings, cut into drumettes and pads

The Buffalo Chicken Wing Sauce (Optional)

- 1/4 cup unsalted margarine

- 1/4 cup Frank's Red-hot Original Cayenne Pepper Sauce

Instructions

- Preheat your Air Fryer whenever prescribed in the manual. Spot the chicken wings in the bin and supplement it into the air fryer.

- Cook the wings for 24 minutes at 380°F (190°C). Shake the bin like clockwork, so they cook uniformly.

- When the time is up, shake the bin, increment the temperature to 400°F (200°C) and cook for six additional minutes or until the skin is brilliant dark colored and firm. Contingent upon the size of your Air Fryer, fresh the wings up in clumps.

- Transfer wings to a bowl and hurl with your most loved BBQ or our simple wild ox wing sauce.

To Make Buffalo Sauce (Optional)

Whisk dissolved spread and hot sauce together in a bowl.

CHAPTER FOUR

SNACKS YOU CAN MAKE IN YOUR NINJAZ FOODY AIR FRYER

Air-Fried Buffalo Cauliflower Bites

Regardless of whether you have vegetarian companions over to watch the game or you simply appreciate recipe blend featuring your preferred flavors, these hot air-singed cauliflower chomps check all the containers. It just takes a dab of blue cheese to add a ton of flavor to the snappy mix together with the sauce.

In case you're not an aficionado of impactful blue cheese, attempt milder gorgonzola, or even feta. To make this straightforward recipe much simpler, get a bundle of pre-cut cauliflower florets.

Ingredients

- 3 tablespoons no-salt-included ketchup
- 2 tablespoons hot sauce, (for example, Franks Red-hot)
- 1 enormous egg white
- 3/4 cup panko (Japanese-style breadcrumbs)
- 1/2 (3-lb.) head cauliflower, cut and cut into 1-inch florets (around 4 cups florets)
- Cooking shower
- 1/4 cup diminished harsh fat cream
- 1/4 ounce disintegrated blue cheese (around 1 Tbsp.)
- 1 little garlic clove, ground
- 1 teaspoon red wine vinegar
- 1/4 teaspoon dark pepper

Step by step instructions to Make It

Step 1

Mix the ketchup, hot sauce, and egg white together in a little bowl until smooth. Spot panko in an enormous bowl. Hurl together cauliflower florets and ketchup blend in a subsequent enormous bowl until covered. Working in clusters, hurl cauliflower in panko to cover. Coat cauliflower well with cooking shower.

Step 2

Spot half of the cauliflower in air fryer bushel, and cook at 320°F until brilliant darker and fresh, around 20 minutes. Rehash with outstanding cauliflower.

Step 3

While cauliflower cooks, mix acrid cream, blue cheese, garlic, vinegar, and pepper in a little bowl. Serve cauliflower with blue cheese sauce.

Air Fryer Sweet Potato Tots

Cooking sweet potato tots in air fryer yields is somewhat fresh outside and a delicate inside. These custom made tots are an extraordinary method to sneak veggies into a fussy eater's meal, in addition to they're more moderate than purchasing pre-made, solidified sweet potato tots.

Splashing the tots with cooking shower assists with caramelizing. However, regardless, they don't darker equally in the air fryer. Make certain to heat the sweet potatoes simply enough that they mesh and hold together when molded, yet at the same time hold a little surface. Not an aficionado of ketchup? Make this Greek yogurt farm dressing.

Ingredients

- 2 little (14 oz. complete) sweet potatoes, stripped
- 1 tablespoon potato starch
- 1/8 teaspoon garlic powder
- 1 1/4 teaspoons legitimate salt, partitioned
- 3/4 cup no-salt-included ketchup
- Cooking splash

The most effective method to Make It

Step 1

Heat a medium pot of water to the point of boiling over high warmth. Include potatoes, and cook until simply fork delicate around 15 minutes. Move potatoes to a plate to cool, around 15 minutes.

Step 2

Working over a medium bowl, grind potatoes utilizing the huge openings of a case grater. Tenderly hurl with potato starch, garlic powder, and 1 teaspoon salt. Shape blend into around 24 (1-inch) tot-molded chambers.

Step 3

Delicately cover air fryer bin with cooking splash. Spot 1/2 of tots (around 12) in a single layer in the crate, and splash with cooking shower. Cook at 400°F until delicately seared, 12 to 14 minutes, turning tots part of the way through cook time. Expel from fry crate and sprinkle with 1/8 teaspoon salt. Rehash with residual tots and salt. Serve promptly with ketchup.

Air Fryer Churros with Chocolate Sauce

These joys are lighter than customary churros—practically like éclairs—leaving the air fryer cushy and delightful. The cinnamon-sugar blend makes a slim hull outwardly, conveying that exemplary churro crunch.

Kefir is a dairy item like yogurt that is a lot more slender (it's drinkable, similar to a smoothie) and stuffed with gut-sound probiotics. The marginally tart flavor makes the chocolate sauce decent and smooth. Make certain to cool the batter before funneling to assist it withholding its shape in the air fryer craze.

You'll to appreciate the churros promptly as they're the best crisp. However, you can spare any additional chocolate sauce—take a stab at showering it over solidified yogurt.

Ingredients

- 1/2 cup water
- 1/4 teaspoon legitimate salt

- 1/4 cup, in addition to 2 Tbsp. unsalted spread, isolated

- 1/2 cup (around 2 1/8 oz.) generally useful flour

- 2 huge eggs

- 1/3 cup granulated sugar

- 2 teaspoons ground cinnamon

- 4 ounces mixed baking chocolate, finely slashed

- 3 tablespoons overwhelming cream

- 2 tablespoons vanilla kefir

The most effective method

Step 1

Bring salt, water, and 1/4 cup of the margarine to a bubble in a little pot over medium-high. Lessen warmth to medium-low; include flour, and mix enthusiastically with a wooden spoon until mixture is smooth around 30 seconds. Keep cooking, always blending, until mixture starts to pull away from sides of the dish and a film frames on the base of the skillet, 2 to 3 minutes. Move mixture to a medium bowl. Mix continually until somewhat cooled, around 1 moment. Include eggs, 1 at once, mixing continuously until totally smooth after every expansion. Move blend to a channeling pack fitted with a medium star tip. Chill 30 minutes.

Step 2

Funnel 6 (3-inch long) pieces in a single layer in air fryer container. Cook at 380°F until brilliant, around 10 minutes. Rehash with remaining batter.

Step 3

Then mix sugar and cinnamon in a medium bowl. Brush cooked churros with staying 2 tablespoons liquefied spread, and move in sugar blend to cover.

Step 4

Spot chocolate and cream in a little microwavable bowl. Microwave on HIGH until liquefied and smooth, around 30 seconds, mixing following 15 seconds. Mix in kefir. Serve churros with chocolate sauce.

Make Loaded Potatoes in an Air Fryer

Solace food just got speedier and simpler graciousness of your air fryer. These fresh potatoes may appear to be liberal, yet brilliant bits of bacon, cheese, and harsh cream include great flavor while holding calories and sat fat in line. The mystery is the inside cut bacon—it concocts decent and firm, and yields simply enough container drippings to make these potatoes truly sparkle. Serve these delicate fresh spuds with a skillet-burned steak and a side of your preferred steamed veggies for a fast and straightforward dinner.

Ingredients

- 11 ounces infant Yukon Gold potatoes (around 8 [2-inch] potatoes)
- 1 teaspoon olive oil
- 2 focus cut bacon cuts
- 1 1/2 tablespoons slashed new chives
- 1/2 ounce finely destroyed diminished fat Cheddar cheese (around 2 Tbsp.)
- 2 tablespoons diminished fat acrid cream
- 1/8 teaspoon fit salt

Step by step instructions to Make It

Step 1

Hurl potatoes with oil to cover. Spot potatoes in air fryer bin, and cook at 350°F until fork delicate, 25 minutes, mixing vegetables once in a while.

Step 2

Cook bacon in a medium skillet over medium until firm, around 7 minutes. Expel bacon from the container; disintegrate. Spot potatoes on a serving platter; softly squash potatoes to part. Sprinkle with bacon drippings. Top with chives, cheese, sharp cream, salt, and disintegrated bacon.

Air-Fried Spicy Chicken Wing Drumettes

Chicken wing drumettes (the top piece of the side) are a savvy decision for air fricasseeing—their little size methods you don't need to go throughout the day cooking unlimited clusters.

Conventional drumettes require vast amounts of oil to ensure most extreme firm goodness; this virtuoso recipe completes it only a tablespoon of super-tasty sesame oil. To get the extra firm, give the drumettes a turn during cooking. Serve these Asian-motivated wings over dark colored rice, or twofold the recipe and fill in as an hors d'oeuvre.

Ingredients

- 10 enormous chicken drumettes
- Cooking shower
- 1/4 cup rice vinegar
- 3 tablespoons nectar
- 2 tablespoons unsalted chicken stock
- 1 tablespoon lower-sodium soy sauce
- 1 tablespoon toasted sesame oil
- 3/8 teaspoon squashed red pepper
- 1 garlic clove, finely slashed

- 2 tablespoons slashed unsalted cooked peanuts

- 1 tablespoon slashed crisp chives

The most effective method to Make It

Step 1

Spot chicken in a single layer in air fryer crate; cover well with cooking splash. Cook at 400°F until the skin is fresh, 30 minutes, turning drumettes over part of the way through cooking.

Step 2

In the interim, mix vinegar, nectar, stock, soy sauce, oil, squashed red pepper, and garlic in a little skillet. Bring to a stew over medium-high; cook until somewhat thickened and practically syrupy, 6 minutes. Spot drumettes in a medium bowl. Include nectar blend, and hurl to cover. Sprinkle with peanuts and chives.

Empanadas in an Air Fryer

Customary meat-filled empanadas can be a one-two punch of fat and calories because of ground hamburger and an excursion to the profound fryer; This air fryer wind is considerably more beneficial gratitude to the expansion of mushrooms, which help the filling while at the same time keeping it pleasant and sodden. We love the productive kind of Castelvetrano olives. However, you can utilize any green olives you have close by. These handheld snacks are extraordinary for closely following, or serve them over greens for a free dinner.

Ingredients

- 1 tablespoon olive oil
- 3 ounces (85/15) lean ground meat
- 1/4 cup finely hacked white onion
- 3 ounces finely chopped cremini mushrooms
- 2 teaspoons finely chopped garlic
- 6 pitted green olives, hacked
- 1/4 teaspoon paprika
- 1/4 teaspoon ground cumin
- 1/8 teaspoon ground cinnamon
- 1/2 cup hacked tomatoes
- 8 square gyoza wrappers
- 1 huge egg, softly beaten

The most effective method to Make It

Step 1

Include meat and onion; cook, blending to disintegrate, until beginning to dark-colored, 3 minutes. Include mushrooms; cook, mixing at times until mushrooms are beginning to dark-colored,

6 minutes. Include garlic, olives, paprika, cumin, and cinnamon; cook until mushrooms are exceptionally delicate and have discharged the more significant part of their fluid, 3 minutes. Mix in tomatoes, and cook one moment, blending sporadically. Move to fill to a bowl, and let cool 5 minutes.

Step 2

Orchestrate four gyoza wrappers on work surface. The spot around 1/2 tablespoons filling in the focus of every wrapper. Brush edges of wrappers with egg; overlap wrappers over, squeezing margins to seal. Rehash process with outstanding wrappers and filling.

Step 3

Spot 4 empanadas in a single layer in air fryer container, and cook at 400°F until pleasantly caramelized 7 minutes. Rehash with remaining empanadas.

Air Fryer Sweet Potato Chips

Sweet potato chips sound like a nutritious tidbit, yet locally acquired adaptations can, in any case, pack critical measures of fat and sodium. Enter air fryer sweet potato chips. These sound custom made chips have 33% of the fat—and they're consummately crunchy and addictive.

If you don't effectively possess a mandoline, this recipe is your reason to get one. This flexible kitchen device makes for exact cutting, which brings about an all the more equitably cooked chip. Furthermore, drenching the sweet potato cuts in water evacuates the starch, making for a crispier chip.

Pack these sweet potato chips into your lunch box or serve them with a smooth plunge, similar to our herby Pesto-Yogurt Dip or this crave-worthy Caramelized Leek and Spinach Dip. What different foods would you be able to air fry? Our assortment of more than 35 sound air fryer recipes has vast amounts of pleasant thoughts from chicken wings to Pop-Tarts to coconut shrimp.

Ingredients

- 1 medium sweet potato, unpeeled, cut into 1/8-inch-thick cuts
- 1 tablespoon canola oil
- 1/4 teaspoon ocean salt
- 1/4 teaspoon newly ground dark pepper
- 1 teaspoon hacked new rosemary (discretionary)
- Cooking splash

The most effective method to Make It

Step 1

In a huge bowl of cold water, splash sweet potato cuts for 20 minutes. Channel sweet potatoes; pat dry with paper towels.

Step 2

Wipe bowl dry; at that point, including oil, salt, pepper, and rosemary (if utilizing). Include sweet potatoes; hurl tenderly to cover.

Step 3

Delicately cover air fryer crate with cooking splash. Spot half of the sweet potatoes in the container and cook in two bunches at 350°F until cooked through and firm, around 15 minutes.

Step 4

Utilizing a pair of tongs, cautiously expel sweet potatoes from air fryer to plate. Let cool; serve quickly or store in an airtight plastic holder.

Oil with Air-Fried Chicken Wings

Try not to fear to overcook these — the more they remain in the air fryer, the more fresh goodness you'll get—indicate ten additional minutes to the cooking time, if you like.

Drumettes have more meat than wings; that is the thing that we use, yet either will work. The crate gets stuffed effectively, so just cook 10 sides one after another, or mix the wings habitually with the goal that they cook uniformly. These wings have a sweet and fiery Asian flavor; sprinkle them with some toasted sesame seeds for additional crunch.

Ingredients

- 10 chicken drumettes (around 1/2 lb.)

- Cooking splash

- 1 tablespoon lower-sodium soy sauce

- 1/2 teaspoon cornstarch

- 2 teaspoons nectar

- 1 teaspoon sambaloelek (ground new bean stew glue)

- 1 teaspoon finely cleaved garlic

- 1/2 teaspoon finely cleaved fresh ginger

- 1 teaspoon new lime juice (from 1 lime)

- 1/8 teaspoon fit salt

- 2 tablespoons slashed scallions

The most effective method to Make It

Step 1

Pat chicken dry with paper towels. Coat chicken well with cooking splash.

Step 2

Spot chicken in air fryer bushel, masterminding drumettes on their sides to abstain from congestion. Cook at 400°F until the skin is exceptionally fresh, 25 minutes, turning drumettes over part of the way through cooking.

Step 3

Mix together soy sauce and cornstarch in a little skillet. Rush in nectar, sambal, garlic, ginger, lime squeeze, and salt. Bring to a stew over medium-high; stew until blend just begins to bubble and is thickened. Spot chicken in a bowl. Include sauce, and hurl to cover. Sprinkle with scallions.

Air Fryer Italian-Style Meatballs

Wet and delicate, these air fryer meatballs are jam-stuffed with enhancing. Cooking them in the air fryer may be outstanding amongst other recipe applications for this gadget. The meatballs are extraordinary all alone; they would likewise be delightful over pasta, rice, or spiralized zoodles. To keep the meatballs from getting over-filled in as you structure them, use what we call the "paw strategy": shape your hand into a hook shape and don't press excessively hard when forming.

Ingredients

- 2 tablespoons olive oil
- 1 medium shallot, minced (around 2 Tbsp.)
- 3 cloves garlic, minced (about 1 Tbsp.)

- 1/4 cup entire wheat panko scraps

- 2 tablespoons entire milk

- 2/3 pound lean ground meat

- 1/3 pound-mass turkey wiener

- 1 huge egg, delicately beaten

- 1/4 cup finely cleaved new level leaf parsley

- 1 tablespoon finely cleaved fresh rosemary

- 1 tablespoon finely cleaved new thyme

- 1 tablespoon Dijon mustard

- 1/2 teaspoon genuine salt

The most effective method to Make It

Step 1

Preheat air-fryer to 400°F. Warmth oil in a medium nonstick container over medium-high warmth. Include shallot and cook until mollified, 1 to 2 minutes. Include garlic and cook just until fragrant, 1 moment. Expel from heat.

Step 2

In a considerable bowl, consolidate panko and milk. Let stand for 5 minutes.

Step 3

Add cooked shallot and garlic to panko blend, alongside meat, turkey frankfurter egg, parsley, rosemary, thyme, mustard, and salt. Mix to join tenderly.

Step 4

Delicately shape blend into 1/2-inch balls. Spot molded balls in a solitary layer in the air-fryer container. Cook a large portion of the meatballs at 400°F until delicately caramelized and cooked through 10 to 11 minutes. Evacuate and keep warm. Rehash with leftover meatballs.

Step 5

Serve warm meatballs with toothpicks as a tidbit or serve over pasta, rice, or spiralized zoodles for a primary dish.

Air Fryer Sweet Potato Fries

Hand-cut fries beat out solidified quickly, and these sweet potato delights are an immense air fryer win. An astounding equalization of delicious and exquisite flavors, these fresh fries get a decent kick of flavor from the garlic and thyme.

They make a decent sound bite or an incredible side with a flame-broiled chicken sandwich or burger.

These fries go incredible with air-singed hot chicken thighs (imagined)! Get the recipe.

Ingredients

- 1 tablespoon olive oil

- 1 teaspoon hacked crisp thyme

- 1/4 teaspoon fine ocean salt

- 1/4 teaspoon garlic powder

- 2 (6-oz.) sweet potatoes, stripped and cut into 1/4-inch sticks

- Cooking splash

How to Make It

Step 1

Mix olive oil, thyme, salt, and garlic powder in a medium bowl. Include sweet potato, and hurl well to cover.

Step 2

Daintily cover air fryer bin with cooking shower. Spot sweet potatoes in a single layer in the container, and cook in clumps at 400°F until delicate within and gently sautéed outwardly, 14 minutes, turning fries over part of the way through cooking.

Whole Wheat Pizzas in an Air Fryer

Notwithstanding conveying solid joys, your air fryer makes a quite marvelous ledge pizza oven. Because of it and this scrumptiously straightforward recipe, Friday pizza night just got epically simpler.

Whole wheat pitas make an extraordinary fiber-forward outside, baking up decent and fresh. Choose Roma tomatoes; their littler size makes them a solid match for these individual pizzas. Swap out fixings to tweak your pizzas; since these cook in only 5 minutes, you can prepare the following one while the first is baking.

Ingredients

- 1/4 cup lower-sodium marinara sauce

- 2 entire wheat pita adjusts

- 1 cup infant spinach leaves (1 oz.)

- 1 little plum tomato, cut into 8 cuts

- 1 small garlic clove, meagerly cut

- 1 ounce pre-destroyed part-skim mozzarella cheese (around 1/4 cup)

- 1/4 ounce shaved Parmigiano-Reggiano cheese (about 1 Tbsp.)

Instructions to Make It

Step 1

Spread marinara sauce uniformly more than 1 side of every pita bread. Top with a large portion of every one of the spinach leaves, tomato cuts, garlic, and cheeses.

Step 2

Spot 1 pita in air fryer container, and cook at 350°F until cheese is softened and pita is fresh, 4 to 5 minutes. Rehash with outstanding pita.

Air Fryer Spanakopita Bites

This is anything your air fryer can't do? Soup, most likely. It would be horrendous at the soup.

Be that as it may, it can shake out these super-crunchy spanakopita nibbles! These delicious Greek phyllo cakes are loaded up with spinach and salty cheeses with only a little hit of lemon and warmth. Exemplary spanakopita calls for brushing the phyllo with margarine; this rendition calls for olive oil, which includes significantly progressively Greek flavor. Loaded up with supplement creamy spinach, these fresh treats make a magnificent gathering dish or hors d'oeuvre.

Ingredients

- 1 (10-oz.) pkg. child spinach leaves

- 2 tablespoons water

- 1/4 cup 1% low-fat curds

- 1-ounce feta cheese, disintegrated (around 1/4 cup)

- 2 tablespoons finely ground Parmesan cheese

- 1 huge egg white

- 1 teaspoon lemon get-up-and-go (from 1 lemon)

- 1 teaspoon dried oregano

- 1/4 teaspoon dark pepper

- 1/4 teaspoon legitimate salt

- 1/8 teaspoon cayenne pepper

- 4 (13-x 18-inch) sheets solidified phyllo batter, defrosted

- 1 tablespoon olive oil

- Cooking splash

The most effective method to Make It

Step 1

Spot spinach and water in a vast pot; cook over high, frequently mixing, until withered, 5 minutes. Channel spinach; cool around 10 minutes. Press solidly with a paper towel to expel, however much dampness as could be expected.

Step 2

Mix spinach, curds, feta cheese, Parmesan cheese, egg white, get-up-and-go, oregano, dark pepper, salt, and cayenne pepper in a medium bowl until all-around mixed.

Step 3

Spot 1 phyllo sheet on work surface. Brush delicately with oil utilizing a cake brush. Top with the second sheet of phyllo; brush with oil. Keep layering to frame a heap of 4 oiled leaves. Working from the long side, cut the stack of phyllo sheets into 8 (2 1/4-inch wide) strips. Cut the pieces down the middle, across, to shape 16 (2 1/4-inch wide) pieces. Spoon around one tablespoon filling onto one short finish of each piece. Overlay one corner over the filling to make a triangle; keep collapsing to and fro to the finish of the piece, making a triangle-molded phyllo parcel.

Step 4

Softly cover air fryer bin with cooking shower. Spot 8 parcels, crease side down, in the bin, daintily shower the tops. Cook at 375°F until phyllo is profound brilliant darker and firm, 12 minutes, turning bundles over part of the way through cooking. Rehash with residual phyllo parcels. Serve warm or at room temperature.

Air-Fried Coconut Shrimp

You can rely on your air fryer to transform an ordinary Friday into a #friyay, particularly if this seashore jump roused recipe is on the menu.

Coconut and panko collaborate to make an incredibly fresh covering for this shrimp; utilize finely destroyed coconut to ensure better outside layer grip. I you can't find finely crushed coconut, beat the coconut in your food processor or give it a quick hack until it's all the more finely ground. Straight from your air fryer and dunked in this sweet-and-tart nectar lime sauce, this addictive application will make you incline that you're on a Caribbean seashore.

Ingredients

- 1/2 cup (around 2 1/8 oz.) universally handy flour

- 1 1/2 teaspoons dark pepper

- 2 enormous eggs

- 2/3 cup unsweetened chipped coconut

- 1/3 cup panko (Japanese-style breadcrumbs)

- 12 ounces medium stripped, deveined crude shrimp, tail-on (around 24 shrimp)

- Cooking shower

- 1/2 teaspoon genuine salt

- 1/4 cup nectar

- 1/4 cup lime juice

- 1 serrano chile, meagerly cut

- 2 teaspoons cleaved crisp cilantro (discretionary)

Step by step instructions to Make It

Step 1

Mix the pepper and flour in a shallow dish. Softly beat eggs in a subsequent shallow bowl. Mix coconut and panko in a third shallow dish. Holding each shrimp by the tail, dig shrimp in flour blend, trying not to cover tail; shake off overabundance. Dunk in egg, enabling any abundance to dribble off. Dig in coconut blend, squeezing to follow. Coat shrimp well with cooking shower.

Step 2

Spot half of the shrimp in air fryer bin, and cook at 400°F until brilliant, 6 to 8 minutes, turning shrimp over part of the way through cooking. Season with 1/4 teaspoon of the salt. Rehash with residual shrimp and salt.

Step 3

While shrimp cook, whisk together nectar, lime juice, and serrano chile in a little bowl. Sprinkle shrimp with cilantro, whenever wanted. Present with sauce.

Crispy Air-Fried Onion Rings With Comeback Sauce

Ok, onion rings—a definitive southern style guilty pleasure.

On account of your air fryer, you can protect this crunchy most loved from the domain of diet expulsion and welcome it back to your plate. These rings of allium greatness leave the air fryer flaunting a brilliantly firm covering with no substantial oiliness.

If you've at any point had rebound sauce, you realize its tart and sweet flavor is the ideal pairing with the crunchy, exquisite onion.

Ingredients

- 1/2 cup (around 2 1/8 oz.) generally useful flour

- 1 teaspoon smoked paprika

- 1/2 teaspoon legitimate salt, separated

- 1 huge egg

- 1 tablespoon water

- 1 cup entire wheat panko (Japanese-style breadcrumbs)

- 1 (10-oz.) sweet onion, cut into 1/2-in.- thick adjusts and isolated into rings

- Cooking shower

- 1/4 cup plain 1% low-fat Greek yogurt

- 2 tablespoons canola mayonnaise

- 1 tablespoon ketchup

- 1 teaspoon Dijon mustard

- 1/4 teaspoon garlic powder

- 1/4 teaspoon paprika

Step by step instructions to Make It

Step 1

Mix flour, smoked paprika, and 1/4 teaspoon of the salt in a shallow dish. Softly beat egg and water in a subsequent shallow dish. Mix panko and staying 1/4 teaspoon salt in a third shallow dish. Dig onion rings in flour blend, shaking off abundance. Dunk in egg blend, enabling any abundance to dribble off. Dig in panko blend, squeezing to follow. Coat the two sides of onion rings well with cooking shower.

Step 2

Spot onion rings in a single layer in air fryer bin, and cook in groups at 375°F until brilliant darker and firm on the two sides, 10 minutes, turning onion rings over part of the way through cooking. Spread to keep warm while cooking the remaining onion rings.

Step 3

In the meantime, mix yogurt, mayonnaise, ketchup, mustard, garlic powder, and paprika in a little bowl until smooth. To serve, place 7 to 7 onion rings on each plate with 2 tablespoons sauce.

Crunchy Air-Fried Corn Dog Bites

Who doesn't cherish a corn hound? These offbeat, ideal little chomps of smoky wiener goodness accompany a crunchy cornflake covering that will make party visitors grin.

Search for high-caliber uncured franks at upscale supermarkets, for example, Whole Foods, Fresh Market, or Sprouts. Mustard is closest companions with corn hounds, so select your most loved to present with these enjoyment and merry snacks.

Ingredients

- 2 uncured all-hamburger franks
- 12 make sticks or bamboo sticks
- 1/2 cup (around 2 1/8 oz.) universally handy flour
- 2 enormous eggs, gently beaten
- 1 1/2 cups finely squashed cornflakes oat
- Cooking shower
- 8 teaspoons yellow mustard

Step by step instructions to Make It

Step 1

Cut each frank into equal parts the long way. Cut every half into 3 equivalent pieces. Addition an art stick or bamboo stick into 1 finish of each bit of frank.

Step 2

Spot flour in a shallow dish. Spot gently beat eggs in a subsequent shallow dish. Spot squashed cornflakes in a third shallow dish. Dig wieners in flour, shaking off abundance. Plunge in egg, enabling any abundance to trickle off. Dig in cornflake morsels, squeezing to follow.

Step 3

Delicately cover air fryer container with cooking splash. Spot 6 corn hound nibbles in a container; gently shower tops with cooking splash. Cook at 375°F until covering is brilliant darker and crunchy, 10 minutes, turning the corn hound nibbles over part of the way through cooking. Rehash with outstanding corn hound nibbles.

Step 4

To serve, place three corn hound chomps on each plate with 2 teaspoons mustard, and serve right away.

Fresh Veggie Quesadillas in an Air Fryer

Filling, however, not substantial, air fryer quesadillas make a fast and fulfilling weeknight dinner. Dark beans carry protein and fiber to the gathering; peppers and zucchini bring shading, crunch, and up your day by day veggie tally. Shop for grew tortillas at well-loaded general stores; customary entire wheat tortillas will work when there's no other option.

Make certain to protect the quesadillas with a toothpick during cooking; the air stream in your fryer can blow them open until the cheese melts and seals everything together. Public Service Announcement: These quesadillas pair flawlessly with super cold lager; limes discretionary.

Ingredients

- 4 (6-in.) grew entire grain flour tortillas
- 4 ounces diminished fat sharp Cheddar cheese, destroyed (around 1 cup)
- 1 cup cut red ringer pepper
- 1 cup cut zucchini
- 1 cup no-salt-included canned dark beans, depleted and flushed
- Cooking shower
- 2 ounces plain 2% diminished fat Greek yogurt

- 1 teaspoon lime pizzazz in addition to 1 Tbsp. crisp juice (from 1 lime)

- 1/4 teaspoon ground cumin

- 2 tablespoons slashed crisp cilantro

- 1/2 cup depleted refrigerated Pico de Gallo

The most effective method to Make It

Step 1

Spot tortillas on a work surface. Sprinkle 2 tablespoons destroyed cheese over portion of every tortilla. Top cheese on every tortilla with 1/4 cup every red pepper cuts, zucchini cuts, and dark beans. Sprinkle uniformly with staying 1/2 cup cheese. Crease tortillas over to frame half-moon formed quesadillas. Delicately cover quesadillas with cooking shower, and secure with toothpicks.

Step 2

Gently shower air fryer container with cooking splash. Cautiously place 2 quesadillas in the bushel, and cook at 400°F until tortillas are brilliant darker and somewhat firm, cheese is liquefied, and vegetables are marginally mollified, 10 minutes, turning quesadillas over part of the way through cooking. Rehash with outstanding quesadillas.

Step 3

While quesadillas cook, mix yogurt, lime pizzazz, lime juice, and cumin in a little bowl. To serve, cut every quesadilla into wedges and sprinkle with cilantro. Serve each with 1 tablespoon cumin cream and 2 tablespoons Pico de Gallo.

Fresh, Sweet Air-Fried Beet Chips

Forte root chips can cost $5 to $6 per pack at the market; spare heaps of cash by preparing a few bunches in your air fryer.

The key to fresh beet chips is to cut the beets very slight; if your blade aptitudes aren't Top Chef level, utilize a mandolin to get skinny cuts. Try not to stuff the bushel; air stream is essential to getting the chips pleasant and firm.

Ingredients

- 3 medium-size red beets (around 1/2 lb.), stripped and cut into 1/8-inch thick cuts (around 3 cups cuts)
- 2 teaspoons canola oil
- 3/4 teaspoon legitimate salt
- 1/4 teaspoon dark pepper

The most effective method to Make It

Step 1

Hurl cut beets, oil, salt, and pepper in a huge bowl.

Step 2

Spot half of the beets in air fryer bushel, and cook at 320°F until dry and fresh, 25 to 30 minutes, shaking the bin like clockwork. Rehash with outstanding beets.

Greek Feta Fries in an Air-Fryer

This dish gets enormous amounts of flavor from the flavors. If your fresh oregano is stable, start with not as much as what's called for and add more to taste. To speed things up, prep every one of the ingredients ahead of time so you can amass rapidly while the fries are as yet hot.

The fries are anything but difficult to make in an air fryer, however on the off chance that you don't have one (yet) no issue: Spread potatoes on a baking sheet covered with cooking shower; prepare 10 minutes at 450F. Flip fries and heat until fresh and dark-colored, another 10-15 minutes.

Ingredients

- Cooking shower

- 2 (7-oz.) Yukon Gold or chestnut potatoes, cleaned and dried

- 1 tablespoon olive oil

- 2 teaspoons lemon pizzazz

- 1/2 teaspoon dried oregano

- 1/4 teaspoon fit salt

- 1/4 teaspoon garlic powder

- 1/4 teaspoon onion powder

- 1/4 teaspoon paprika

- 1/4 teaspoon dark pepper

- 2 ounces feta cheese, finely ground (around 1/2 cup)

- 2 ounces destroyed skinless rotisserie chicken bosom

- 1/4 cup arranged tzatziki

- 1/4 cup seeded and diced plum tomato

- 2 tablespoons slashed red onion

- 1 tablespoon slashed crisp level leaf parsley and oregano

Step by step instructions to Make It

Step 1

Preheat an air fryer to 380°F. Coat the container with a cooking shower.

Step 2

Cut every potato the long way into 1/4-inch-thick cuts; cut each cut into 1/4-inch fries.

Step 3

Hurl together the potatoes and oil in an enormous bowl. Season with get-up-and-go, dried oregano, salt, garlic powder, onion powder, paprika, and pepper; hurl to cover.

Step 4

In 2 clusters, cook the prepared potatoes until fresh, around 15 minutes, flipping fries part of the way through cooking time.

Step 5

Return the leading group of fries to the crate, and cook until warmed through 1 to 2 minutes. Expel from air fryer. Top chips with half of the feta, chicken, tzatziki, remaining feta, tomato, red onion, and new herbs.

Air Fryer Potato Chips

The firm, crunchy, and addictive, air fryer potato chips have 60 percent less fat than their locally acquired partners. Indeed, making potato contributes your air fryer requires a smidgen of exertion—yet the outcome is a salty bite that is, in reality, entirely sound. Shows improvement over that?

Acing air fryer potato chips takes practice—and you'll need to keep an eye on the part of the way through cooking, at that point all the more as often as possible towards the finish of their cooking cycle. Use tongs to painstakingly isolate any chips that have adhered to one another to guarantee they cook uniformly, and expel any disks that are completely crisped.

Make a group of these chips for your next gathering, and serve them with our rich tart Miso-Ranch Dip. Prepared to get on board with the air fryer temporary fad? Look at these 35 reliable air fryer recipes for scrumptious thoughts from chicken wings to corn hound nibbles.

Ingredients

- 1 medium Russet potato, unpeeled, cut into 1/8 inch thick cuts (around 3/4 pound)

- 1 tablespoon canola oil

- 1/4 teaspoon ocean salt

- 1/4 teaspoon naturally ground dark pepper

- Canola oil

- 1 teaspoon slashed new rosemary

Fresh, crunchy, and addictive, air fryer potato chips have 60 percent less fat than their locally acquired partners. Indeed, making potato contributes your air fryer requires a tad of exertion—however, the outcome is a salty bite that is, in reality, quite solid. Shows improvement over that?

Step by step instructions to Make It

Step 1

In an enormous bowl of cold water, drench potato cuts for 20 minutes. Channel potatoes; pat dry with paper towels.

Step 2

Wipe bowl dry; at that point, including oil, salt, and pepper. Include potatoes; hurl delicately to cover.

Step 3

Softly cover air fryer bin with cooking splash. Spot half of the potato cuts in the container and cook in two groups at 375°F until cooked through and firm, around 25 to 30 minutes.

Step 4

Utilizing a pair of tongs, cautiously expel chips from air fryer to plate. Sprinkle over rosemary; serve promptly or store in an airtight plastic compartment.

Air-Fried Pork Dumplings with Dipping Sauce

Asian dumplings are an astonishing hors d'oeuvre—the ideal mix of firm and chewy. Nothing unexpected here: Your air fryer can shake this recipe like a champ.

Pork and ginger are the stars enhance in these tasty little chomps, alongside snappy sautéed bouchon. These simple to-amass appetizers make an incredible family cooking undertaking—only stuff, seal, and air-fry your approach to custom made takeout goodness. Search for little dumpling wrappers at Asian markets; ordinary egg move wrappers will work after all other options have been exhausted.

Ingredients

- 1 teaspoon canola oil

- 4 cups slashed bouchon (around 12 oz.)

- 1 tablespoon slashed crisp ginger

- 1 tablespoon slashed garlic (3 garlic cloves)

- 4 ounces ground pork

- 1/4 teaspoon squashed red pepper

- 18 (3 1/2-inch-square) dumpling wrappers or wonton wrappers

- Cooking shower

- 2 tablespoons rice vinegar

- 2 teaspoons lower-sodium soy sauce

- 1 teaspoon toasted sesame oil

- 1/2 teaspoon pressed light darker sugar

- 1 tablespoon finely slashed scallions

The most effective method to Make It

Step 1

Warmth canola oil in a substantial nonstick skillet over medium-high. Include bouchon, and cook, frequently mixing, until withered and generally dry, 6 to 8 minutes. Include ginger and garlic; cook, always mixing, 1 moment. Move bouchon blend to a plate to cool 5 minutes. Pat the combination dry with a paper towel.

Step 2

Mix ground pork, bouchon blend, and squashed red pepper in a medium bowl.

Step 3

Spot a dumpling wrapper on a work surface, and spoon around 1 tablespoon filling in the focus of wrapper. Utilizing a cake brush or your fingers, daintily soak the edges of the wrapper with water. Overlap the wrapper over to make a half-moon shape, squeezing margins to seal. Rehash process with outstanding wrappers and filling.

Step 4

Delicately cover air fryer bin with cooking shower. Spot 6 dumplings in the container, leaving room between each; daintily splash the dumplings with cooking shower. Cook at 375°F until gently seared, 12 minutes, turning meatballs over partially through cooking. Rehash with outstanding dumplings, keeping cooked dumplings warm.

Step 5

Then, mix rice vinegar, soy sauce, sesame oil, darker sugar, and scallions in a little bowl until sugar is disintegrated. To serve, place 3 dumplings on each plate with 2 teaspoons sauce.

Air-Fried Curry Chickpeas

The fundamental element of hummus, rich chickpeas, prepares into fresh little chunks in the blink of an eye. These are an incredible bite substitute for chips because of heaps of fiber and a decent measure of protein. Be delicate when pounding the chickpeas in step 1; you need to squeeze them sufficiently only to get the external skin to discharge, rather than squashing them into the glue. If you can't find Aleppo pepper, utilize 1/4 tsp. squashed red pepper pieces. You can make these ahead; they'll keep about seven days in an airtight holder.

Ingredients

- 1 (15-oz.) can no-salt-included chickpeas (garbanzo beans), depleted and washed (around 1/2 cups)

- 2 tablespoons red wine vinegar

- 2 tablespoons olive oil

- 2 teaspoons curry powder

- 1/2 teaspoon ground turmeric

- 1/4 teaspoon ground coriander

- 1/4 teaspoon ground cumin

- 1/4 teaspoon in addition to 1/8 tsp. ground cinnamon

- 1/4 teaspoon genuine salt

- 1/2 teaspoon Aleppo pepper

- Thinly cut new cilantro

Instructions to Make It

Step 1

Tenderly crush chickpeas with your hands in a medium bowl (don't pulverize); dispose of chickpea skins.

Step 2

Add vinegar and oil to chickpeas, and hurl to cover. Include curry powder, turmeric, coriander, cumin, and cinnamon; mix delicately to join.

Step 3

Spot chickpeas in a single layer in air fryer bushel, and cook at 400°F until fresh, around 15 minutes, shaking chickpeas part of the way through cooking.

Step 4

Move chickpeas to a bowl. Sprinkle with salt, Aleppo pepper, and cilantro; hurl to cover.

Air-Fried "Everything Bagel" Kale Chips

These flavor-stuffed nutritious chips leave the air fryer much crispier than they do from your standard oven.

Locally acquired, everything bagel flavoring can be pigged out with sodium. Our natively constructed rendition conveys a similar flavor utilizing staples you most likely have hanging out in your zest bureau. Shop for the perkiest new kale you can put your hands on—it yields the crispiest chips.

Ingredients

- 6 cups stuffed torn Lacinato kale leaves, stems and ribs evacuated

- 1 tablespoon olive oil

- 1 teaspoon lower-sodium soy sauce

- 1 teaspoon white or dark sesame seeds

- 1/2 teaspoon dried minced garlic

- 1/4 teaspoon poppy seeds

The most effective method to Make It

Step 1

Wash and dry kale leaves, and attack 1/2-inch pieces. Hurl together kale, olive oil, and soy sauce in a medium bowl, scouring the leaves tenderly to be certain they are very much covered with the blend.

Step 2

Spot 33% of the kale leaves in the air fryer container and cook at 375°F until fresh, 6 minutes, shaking bin part of the way through cooking. Spot kale chips on a baking sheet, and sprinkle equally with sesame seeds, garlic, and poppy seeds while still hot. Rehash with residual kale leaves.

Shrimp Spring Rolls with Sweet Chili Sauce

Crunch is the name of the game with these shrimp-and veggie-pressed spring rolls.

Crisp carrots and cabbage hold their surface pleasantly in the air fryer, and the shrimp includes a decent top you-off factor. Make certain to buy slim spring move wrappers (not thicker egg move wrappers) and brush them with oil before cooking to get the crispiest outcomes.

Ingredients

- 2 1/2 tablespoons sesame oil, separated

- 2 cups pre-destroyed cabbage

- 1 cup matchstick carrots

- 1 cup julienne-cut red chime pepper

- 4 ounces stripped, deveined crude shrimp, hacked

- 3/4 cup julienne-cut snow peas

- 1/4 cup hacked crisp cilantro

- 1 tablespoon new lime juice

- 2 teaspoons fish sauce

- 1/4 teaspoon squashed red pepper

- 8 (8-inch-square) spring move wrappers

- 1/2 cup sweet bean stew sauce

Step by step instructions to Make It

Step 1

Warmth 1/2 teaspoons of the oil in an enormous skillet over high until marginally smoking. Include cabbage, carrots, and chime pepper; cook, always mixing until delicately dried, 1 to 1/2 minutes. Spread on a rimmed baking sheet; cool 5 minutes.

Step 2

Spot cabbage blend, shrimp, snow peas, cilantro, lime juice, fish sauce, and squashed red pepper in an enormous bowl; hurl to join.

Step 3

Spot spring moves wrappers on a work surface with 1 corner confronting you. Spoon 1/4 cup filling in the focus of each spring move wrapper, spreading from left to directly into a 3-inch long strip. Overlay base corner of every wrapper over filling, tucking tip of corner under filling. Overlap left and right corners overfilling. Softly brush remaining corner with water; firmly roll filled end toward residual corner; delicately press to seal. Brush spring moves with staying 2 tablespoons oil.

Step 4

Spot 4 spring abounds in air fryer bin, and cook at 390°F until brilliant, 6 to 7 minutes, turning spring moves following 5 minutes. Rehash with outstanding spring rolls. Present with sweet bean stew sauce.

Air Fryer Pizza

Impeccably firm, simple to make, individual dish pizzas that are going to reform pizza night.

Ingredients

- Buffalo mozzarella

- Pizza batter 1 12-inch mixture will make 2 individual measured pizzas

- Olive oil

- Tomato sauce

- Optional fixings to complete: crisp basil, parmesan cheese, pepper drops

Instructions

Prep: Preheat air fryer to 375°F (190°C). Splash air fryer container well with oil. Pat mozzarella dry with paper towels (to forestall a saturated pizza).

Amass: Roll out pizza mixture to the size of your air fryer container. Cautiously move it to the air fryer, at that point, brush softly with a teaspoon or so of olive oil. Spoon on a light layer of tomato sauce and sprinkle with lumps of wild ox mozzarella.

Heat: For around 7 minutes until the covering is fresh and cheese has dissolved. Alternatively, top with basil, ground parmesan, and pepper chips just before serving.

Air Fryer Brussels Sprouts

Air singing Brussels grows cooks them rapidly. However, they become impeccably, brilliant dark colored and firm. Here's how to cook Brussels grows in your air fryer!

Brussels Sprout Seasoning Ideas

You can season this simmered Brussels grows with your preferred seasonings and fixings! Below are a couple of our top choices:

- **Garlic:** part of the way through cooking, hurl the Brussels grows with a couple of cloves of minced garlic.

- **Balsamic**: Drizzle balsamic decrease (a thickened balsamic vinegar) over the Brussels grows just before serving.

- **Parmesan**: Grated parmesan cheese is additionally delightful sprinkled over the cooked Brussels grows!

- **No Oil:** You can air fry this Brussels grows with no or less oil (however, I do suggest utilizing some oil for the flavor). To utilize less oil, splash the sprouts with oil to equitably cover while utilizing less. To utilize no oil discard it from the recipe.

Ingredients

- ½ lb. Brussels grows 2 to 3 cups

- 1 Tbsp olive oil 15 mL

- Pinch salt and pepper

- Optional: garlic, balsamic decrease, parmesan cheese

Instructions

Prep: Remove the extreme parts of the bargains sprouts and expel any harmed external leaves. Wash under virus water and pat dry. If your sprouts are on the enormous side, cut them down the middle. Hurl in oil, salt, and pepper.

Cook: Arrange Brussels grows in a solitary layer in your air fryer, working in bunches on the off chance that they don't all fit. Cook at 375°F (190°C) for 8 to 12 minutes, shaking the dish part of the way through cooking to equitably darker them. They are down when gently seared and firm on the edges.

Serve: Serve grows warm, alternatively beat with balsamic decrease and parmesan.

Notes

Minor departure from this recipe:

- **Garlic**: part of the way through cooking, hurl the sprouts with a couple of cloves of minced garlic.

- **Balsamic:** Drizzle on balsamic decrease just before serving.

- **Parmesan:** Sprinkle over the cooked sprouts.

- **No Oil:** You can air fry this Brussels grows with no or less oil (however, I do prescribe utilizing some oil for the flavor). To utilize less oil, splash the sprouts with oil to equally cover while utilizing less. To utilize no oil, just overlook it from the recipe.

- **Frozen:** To air-fry solidified Brussels grows, space the sprouts out additional in the air fryer to enable abundance dampness to dissipate, at that point add 3 to 5 minutes to the cooking time.

Firm Air Fried Tofu

No cornstarch expected to make this delectably fresh tofu recipe! This vegetarian air seared tofu possesses a flavor like it's directly from the profound fryer (while being route lower in fat).

Fresh Tofu Ingredients

There are two principle segments to this fresh tofu: the tofu (duh), and the marinade.

- **Tofu:** Use extra-firm tofu, which has more water crushed out of it than the delicate or smooth assortments. Less water = progressively fresh!

- **Soy sauce**: Soy (or tamari for sans gluten) includes a rich and salty flavor that steps up your tofu.

- Oil: We'll utilize a mix of sesame/olive oil to include flavor and upgrade the firmness. I wouldn't suggest removing the oil. However, you could utilize sprayable oil in case you're hoping to decrease fat.

- **Garlic:** I utilize this for snappy and basic flavor in the marinade. Don't hesitate to go insane with it and at your mix of flavors or herbs!

- **A tofu press:** You'll need to squeeze water out of your tofu before cooking it.

Ingredients

- 1 16-oz square extra-firm tofu 453 g

- 2 Tbsp soy sauce 30 mL

- 1 Tbsp toasted sesame oil 15 mL

- 1 Tbsp olive oil 15 mL

- 1 clove garlic minced

Instructions

Press: Press tofu for 15 minutes, utilizing either a tofu press or by setting a substantial dish over it, allowing the dampness to moisture. At the point when completed, cut tofu into reduced down squares and move to a bowl.

Flavor: Combine every single outstanding fixing in a little bowl. Sprinkle over tofu and hurl to cover. Let tofu marinate for an extra 15 minutes.

Air Fry: Preheat your air fryer to 375 degrees F (190 C). Add tofu squares to your air fryer crate in a solitary layer. Cook for 10 to 15 minutes, shaking the skillet every so often to advance in any event, cooking.

Buttermilk Fried Mushrooms

This Buttermilk Fried Mushrooms formula is going to alter your veggie lover cooking. With air singed clam mushrooms and a crunchy covering, it tastes simply like seared chicken!

Ingredients

- 2 stacking cups shellfish mushrooms

- 1 cup of buttermilk 240 mL, see notes for veggie lover substitute

- 1 1/2 cups generally useful flour 200 g

- 1 tsp each salt, pepper, smoked paprika, garlic powder, onion powder, and cumin

- 1 Tbsp oil

Directions

Marinate: Air fryer to 375 degrees F (190 C). Clean mushrooms at that point hurl together with buttermilk in a huge bowl. Let marinate for 15 minutes.

Breading: In a huge bowl, join flour and flavors. Spoon mushrooms out of the buttermilk (spare the buttermilk). Dunk each mushroom in the flour blend, shake off abundance flour, plunge again in the buttermilk, at that point in the flour (in short: wet > dry > wet > dry).

Cook: Grease the base of your air fry container well. At that point, place mushrooms in a solitary layer, leaving space between mushrooms. Cook for 5 minutes, at that point, generally brush all sides with a little oil to advance sautéing. Keep cooking 5 to 10 additional minutes, until brilliant dark colored and fresh.

Notes

- Make veggie-lover buttermilk by consolidating 1/2 Tbsp lemon juice + 1/2 cups plain soy milk.

- Alternatively, spritz with cooking shower for even inclusion and less in general oil.

Fresh Avocado Tacos

Velvety, firm vegan avocado tacos with new pineapple salsa and a smooth chipotle sauce.

Elements for these Avocado Tacos

- Avocados: Breaded with panko then either heated or air seared into fresh flawlessness.

- Pineapple Salsa: We'll make snappy pineapple salsa, however, don't hesitate to sub your preferred locally acquired salsa!

- Creamy Chipotle Sauce: A straightforward combo of yogurt, mayo, and adobo sauce (from a container of chipotle peppers).

Ingredients

Salsa (can sub your preferred locally acquired)

- 1 cup finely cleaved or squashed pineapple 240 g
- 1 Roma tomato finely cleaved
- 1/2 red ringer pepper finely cleaved
- 1 clove garlic minced
- 1/2 jalapeno finely cleaved
- Pinch every cumin and salt

Avocado Tacos

- 1 avocado
- 1/4 cup universally handy flour 35 g
- 1 enormous egg whisked
- 1/2 cup panko scraps 65 g
- Pinch each salt and pepper
- 4 flour tortillas click for formula

Adobo Sauce

- 1/4 cup plain yogurt 60 g

- 2 Tbsp mayonnaise 30 g

- 1/4 tsp lime juice

- 1 Tbsp adobo sauce from a container of chipotle peppers

Guidelines

Salsa: Combine all Salsa fixings (finely slash by hand or barrage in the nourishment processor), spread, and set in the ice chest.

Prep Avocado: Cut avocado into equal parts the long way and evacuate pit. Spot avocado skin side down and cut every half into 4 equivalent estimated pieces, at that point delicately strip the skin off of each.

Prep Station: Preheat grill to 450 F (230 C) or air fryer to 375 F (190 C). Mastermind your workspace, so you have a bowl of flour, a bowl of whisked egg, a bowl of panko with S&P blended in, and material lined heating sheet toward the end.

Coat: Dip every avocado cut first in the flour, at that point egg, at that point panko. Spot on the readied heating sheet and either prepare or air fry for 10 minutes, flipping part of the way through cooking, until softly caramelized.

Sauce: While avocados are cooking, consolidate all Sauce fixings.

Serve: Spoon salsa onto a tortilla, and top with two bits of avocado, and shower with sauce. Serve quickly and appreciate it!

The most effective method to Air Fry Any Vegetable

Your definitive manual for air fryer vegetables! Step by step instructions to air fry essentially any vegetable into superbly cooked, solid heavenliness.

Ingredients

Delicate vegetables

- Crucifers broccoli, cauliflower, Brussels grows
- Soft Veggies like chime pepper, tomato
- Thin Veggies like asparagus

Firm vegetables

- Root Vegetable carrots, beets, potato, parsnip
- Winter Squash butternut, oak seed, pumpkin

Solidified vegetables

• Any of the veggies from above

Directions

Delicate Veggies: Preheat air fryer to 375 degrees F (190 C). Prep veggies by hacking them to the size you need, alternatively showering with oil (this will make them more cooked tasting at last). Add to your air fryer in as level of a layer as would be prudent and cook for 10 to 15 minutes, shaking the air fryer container more than once during cooking to advance in any event, cooking.

Firm Veggies: Preheat air fryer to 375 degrees F (190 C). Prep veggies by cleaving them to the size you need (recall: littler pieces cook quicker!) Optionally sprinkle with oil and add to your air fryer in as level of a layer as could be allowed. Cook for 20 to 30 minutes, shaking the air fryer dish a couple of times during cooking to advance in any event, cooking.

Solidified Veggies: Figure out which classification your veggie falls under (delicate or firm). At that point, simply add a couple of moments to the cooking time to represent the veggies defrosting during the cooking procedure. Make certain to give space between your veggies to guarantee they become splendidly cooked.

Crispy Air Fryer Chickpeas

Crispy Air Fryer Chickpeas are my go-to nibble. They're scrumptious, crunchy, filling, and delectable. To make this formula, you'll need only 15 minutes.

Ingredients for Crispy Air Fryer Cauliflower

In the same way as other of my air fryer plans, this one requires negligible fixings to accomplish a tasty, crunchy result. It calls for three primary fixings:

- **Chickpeas:** We will utilize one jar of chickpeas to make this firm tidbit. For best outcomes, pat them dry with a paper towel before air browning.

- **Olive Oil**: Olive oil is utilized to cover the chickpeas. It enables the seasonings to stick, and makes them firm!

- **Salt:** Salt is an incredible, exemplary flavoring decision that preferences heavenly with chickpeas.

- **Seasoning of Your Choice**: Feel allowed to blend it up by dumping the salt and utilizing your favored flavoring. See underneath for Ranch, Dorito, and coconut curry thoughts!

Ingredients

- 1 14-oz can chickpeas 425g

- 1 Tbsp olive oil 15 mL

- ½ tsp salt or flavoring of decision, see notes

Directions

- Prep: Drain and pat chickpeas dry with a paper towel. Hurl together with oil and salt (or your picked flavoring).

- Cook: Spread in a solitary layer in your air fryer crate or rack. Cook at 390°F (200°C) for 8 to 10 minutes, or until fresh and delicately sautéed.

Notes

- **Optional flavorings:** Toss on before heating. A couple of my top choices:

- Ranch: ½ tsp dried dill, ½ tsp dried chives, ½ tsp garlic powder, ½ tsp onion powder, ¼ tsp salt, ¼ tsp pepper

- Dorito: 2 Tbsp wholesome yeast, ¼ tsp garlic powder, ¼ tsp onion powder, ¼ tsp cumin, ¼ tsp paprika, ¼ tsp bean stew powder, ¼ tsp salt

- Coconut Curry: 1 Tbsp unsweetened destroyed coconut, ½ tsp curry powder, ¼ tsp salt

- Store these simmered chickpeas in a paper pack, or an approximately fixed plastic sack fixed with a paper towel. They keep well at room temperature for as long as seven days.

- Serve on Roasted Chickpea Gyros, in Chickpea Stuffed Avocados, or as a garnish for Pumpkin Soup!

Air Fryer Fried Chicken

This Air Fryer singed chicken is a more advantageous and simpler form of conventional seared chicken. Absorbed buttermilk and hot sauce, shrouded in prepared flour, and air seared to flawlessness.

Ingredients

Marinade

- ½ entire chicken cut into independent pieces (bosom, thigh, wing, and leg)
- ½ cup hot sauce
- ½ cup buttermilk

Flavoring

- ¾ cup All-Purpose Flour
- 2 tsp flavoring salt
- 1 tsp garlic powder
- 1 tsp onion powder
- 1 tsp Italian flavoring
- ½ tsp cayenne pepper
- Oil for splashing Canola or Vegetable

Directions

Spot chicken pieces in buttermilk and hot sauce. The spot in cooler and permit to marinate whenever from 1-24 hours.

Whisk together universally handy flour, flavoring salt, garlic powder, onion powder, Italian flavoring, and cayenne pepper in a bowl. Put in a safe spot.

Place a material liner in the Air Fryer bin.

Expel a bit of chicken from the buttermilk blend and spot in the flour blend, covering all sides of the chicken and shaking off any abundance flour. Spot the chicken pieces in the bin in a solitary layer.

Close the Air Fryer container and set the temperature to 390 degrees Fahrenheit and clock to 25 minutes. Start the Air Fryer.

Following 13 minutes, open the air fryer and shower any flour spots on the chicken. Flip the chicken and splash the opposite side with oil, guaranteeing all the flour spots are secured. Close the air fryer and cook for 12 additional minutes.

When the clock is up, open the Air Fryer and check chicken pieces with a snappy read thermometer. Chicken is done when it arrives at an inside temperature of 165 degrees at the thickest piece of the chicken.

Notes

- I don't suggest covering the chicken pieces in this formula. It's ideal to have the chicken spaces in a solitary layer and not contacting. That way, the air can get around the chicken to fresh it up and give it that pleasant and firm brilliant layer.

- Remember to splash delicately with oil. The motivation behind the oil in this formula is to cover the dried flour spots. Not splashing with oil will have those flour spots posing a flavor like you would envision they would, dry flour.

- Some breading will fall off, regardless of whether you utilize the liners or not. Be that as it may, considerably less breading falls of when utilizing the material liners.

- If utilizing material liners, ensure that you place the chicken over them before beginning the Air Fryer. Not doing so will make the liners fly into the fan, get captured, and potentially light a fire.

- Timing will change contingent upon the Air Fryer brand. Utilize a meat thermometer to guarantee your chicken has, in any event, arrived at a temperature of 165 degrees Fahrenheit. My chicken, as a rule, arrives at 180 degrees or more is as yet succulent and delicious crisp.

- This chicken is best to serve that day. On the off chance that warming, place chicken in Air Fryer and cook on 370 for around 10 minutes.

- Use any piece of the chicken you like that has skin on. The breading may not adhere to skinless chicken, and it may not be as fresh.

Air Fryer Whole Chicken

This Air Fryer Whole Chicken is so straightforward and flavorful. In no time, you can have a delicious and delicate chicken, with an overwhelming fresh skin. You'll never need to purchase a market rotisserie chicken again!

Ingredients

- 2 tbsp spread, relaxed
- 1 entire chicken, around 3-5 pounds
- 2 tbsp BBQ Rub and Seasoning, or bar-b-que rub of your decision

Directions

Expel chicken from bundling and pat dry with paper towels. Expel and dispose of neck and giblets from the cavity of the chicken.

Extricate skin from the bosom meat of the chicken by running a little spatula or your fingers delicately underneath the skin. Spread 2 tablespoons of mollified margarine underneath the skin on the two bosoms. Utilize your fingers to spread it around under the skin.

Generously sprinkle the bar-b-que flavoring over all sides of the chicken and rub into the skin with the goal that it sticks. Spot the entire chicken bosom side down in the bushel of your air fryer.

Set the air fryer to 350 degrees and cook the chicken for 30 minutes. Following 30 minutes is up, pull out the crate and flip the chicken bosom side up. Spot back noticeable all around fryer at 350 degrees for 15-25 minutes, or until a meat thermometer arrives at 165 degrees.

Enable chicken to rest for around 10 minutes before serving. Appreciate!

Air Fryer Rotisserie Chicken
Ingredients

- 1 Whole Chicken cleaned and smudged dry

- 2 Tablespoons Ghee (or excellent Coconut Oil or Olive Oil)

- 1 Tablespoon

Guidelines

- Remove giblet parcel from chicken and pat-dry.

- Rub Ghee/Oil all over chicken and season liberally.

- Place chicken, bosom side down into Air Fryer bin.

- Cook at about 350 degrees for 30 minutes.

- Flip chicken over and cook for 350 degrees for an extra 30 minutes, or until inside temperature arrives at 165 degrees.

- Let rest for 10 minutes and afterward serve.

Notes

For chickens that are five pounds and up, utilize a 5.8 quart or bigger Air Fryer can cook for 35 minutes on each side.

If utilizing the Ninjaz foody to air fry in the Instant Pot, MealthyMultiPot or Pressure Cooker utilize the short-legged trivet and the crisp lid bushel is discretionary.

If utilizing an air fryer stove, there is no compelling reason to turn over the chicken (as a rule).

Air Fryer Donuts 2 Ways

Air Fryer Donuts are a more advantageous rendition of your preferred sweet treat that is fun and simple to make!

Ingredients

From Scratch Way:

- 2 cups universally handy flour

- 1/4 cup granulated sugar

- 1.5 tsp quick activity yeast

- ¼ tsp ground nutmeg

- salt

- 1/2 cup entire milk at room temperature

- 2 tbsp unsalted margarine liquefied

- 1 enormous egg beaten

Simple Biscuit Way:

• 1 jar of bread rolls 8 scones, flaky kind

Coating:

- 1 cup (around 4 oz) powdered sugar

- 4 tsp faucet water

- various sprinkles and palatable dried blooms

Instructions

To Make the From Scratch Way:

- Combine flour, sugar, yeast, nutmeg, and salt in a bowl.

- Add in the milk, margarine, and egg and mix into a delicate mixture.

- Place doughnut mixture onto a gently floured surface and ply for two or three mins until smooth.

- Transfer it to a softly oiled bowl, spread it, and let ascend in a warm spot until multiplied in size.

- Turn mixture out onto a gently floured surface and turn out to 1/4-inch thickness.

- Cut out 7-8 doughnuts utilizing a 3-inch round shaper. At that point, utilize a 1-inch round shaper to evacuate focus.

- Place both the doughnuts and doughnuts openings on a gently floured surface spread freely with a piece of fabric and let remain in a warm spot until multiplied in size (roughly 30 mins).

- Pre-heat air fryer to 350F/180C and splash the crate with cooking shower.

- Place a portion of the doughnuts in a single layer inside the air fryer bushel and cook for 4-5 mins until brilliant. Rehash with outstanding doughnuts and gaps.

To Make The Super Easy Biscuit Way:

- Lay the bread rolls on a level surface. Utilize a little (1-inch) round cutout to evacuate focus.

- Pre-heat air fryer to 350F/180C and shower the air fryer bushel with cooking splash.

- Place the doughnuts in a solitary layer inside the air fryer bin (don't stack) and softly shower the doughnuts with oil.

- Cook for 4-5 mins until brilliant. Rehash with residual doughnuts and openings.

To Make The Glaze:

- Mix the powdered sugar with water in a bowl until smooth.

- Dip the doughnuts and doughnut openings in the sugar coat. At that point, place them on a wire rack set over a rimmed baking sheet to enable abundance coating to dribble off.

- Top doughnuts with sprinkles and eatable blooms.

- Let doughnuts remain until coat solidifies (around 10 mins) before serving.

Air Fryer Blueberry Hand Pies

These Air Fryer Blueberry Hand Pies are flavorful, lovable, and versatile.

Ingredients

- 1 cup (128g) blueberries

- 2.5 tbsp caster sugar

- 1 tsp lemon juice

- 1 squeeze salt

- 14 ounces (320g) refrigerated pie outside layer or short crust cake roll

- water

- vanilla sugar to sprinkle on top (discretionary)

Instructions

Air Fryer Version:

- Mix the blueberries, sugar, lemon squeeze, and salt in a medium bowl.

- Roll out the piecrusts (or short crust baked good roll) and cut out 6-8 (4-inch) singular circles.

- Place around one tablespoon of the blueberry filling in the focal point of each circle.

- Moisten edges of the mixture with water, and crease the batter over the filling to frame a half-moon shape.

- Using a fork, delicately crease the edges of the piecrust together. At that point, cut three cuts on the highest point of the hand pies.

- Spray the hand pies with cooking shower and sprinkle with vanilla sugar (if utilizing).

- Preheat the air fryer to.

- Place the 3-4 hand pies in a single layer inside the air fryer container.

- Cook for 9-12 mins, or until brilliant darker.

- Let the pies cool for at any rate 10 mins before serving.

Oven Version:

- Mix blueberries, sugar, lemon squeeze, and salt in a medium bowl and put in a safe spot.

- Roll out the piecrusts (or short crust cake roll) and cut out into 6-8 (4-inch) circles.

- Place around 1 tablespoon of the blueberry filling in the focal point of each circle.

- Moisten edges of batter with water and overlay mixture over the filling to frame a half-moon shape.

- Use a fork and tenderly crease the edges of the piecrust together. At that point, cut three cuts on the highest point of the hand pies.

- Spray the hand pies with a cooking splash and sprinkle with vanilla sugar (if utilizing).

- Preheat oven to fan helped 180 C/200C/400F/gas 6.

- Transfer hand pies to a lined baking sheet.

- Bake in the preheated oven until the pies are brilliant dark-colored and filling is foaming, 25 to 30 mins.

- Let the pies cool for in any event 10 mins before serving.

Tips for Making Air Fryer Blueberry Hand Pies

- Since air fryer temperatures can differ contingent upon the make and model, this recipe incorporates a scope of proposed cook times. I prescribe beginning with less time, checking for doneness, and afterward, including additional time-varying.

- For those with dietary limitations, you can make these hand pies utilizing arranged gluten-free or veggie lover piecrust.

- Vary the filling flavor by swapping the blueberries for raspberries or blackberries. Different tasty filling renditions incorporate finely-hacked apple and cinnamon, or chocolatey Nutella.

Air Fryer Apple Chips

Air Fryer Apple Chips are an enjoyment, kid-accommodating, and sound tidbit.

Ingredients

- 1 apple

- ¼ tsp ground cinnamon

- Pinch of salt

Instructions

Air Fryer Version:

- Preheat the air fryer to 360 F/180C.

- Thinly cut the apples utilizing either a mandolin or a sharp blade.

- Add apples to bowl and consolidate with cinnamon and salt.

- Transfer portion of the spiced apple cuts to the air fryer crate, masterminding in a solitary layer.

- Cook for 8-10 minutes, turning and smoothing them, in any event, multiple times during the cooking procedure.

- Remove the cooked apples chips and afterward rehash with the remainder of the apple cuts.

Oven Version:

- Preheat oven to 225 F/110 C.

- Thinly cut the apples utilizing either a mandolin or a sharp blade.

- Add apples to bowl and consolidate with cinnamon and salt.

- Arrange apple cuts on a metal baking sheet.

- Bake for a 45-an hour until apples are evaporated and edgy twist.

- Using a spatula, move the apple chips onto a wire rack until completely cooled and firm.

Tips for Making Air Fryer Apple Chips

- Using a mandolin to cut the apples works best. However, if that isn't an alternative, make a point to utilize a sharp blade.

- Try to ensure the apple cuts are no different thickness so they will cook at a similar rate.

- If they are not any different size, isolate into groups as per thickness, and cook comparable size cuts together.

- If a few cuts are cooking faster than others, just expel the speedier cooking ones prior.

- Air fryer temperatures can differ contingent upon the make and model, so this recipe incorporates a scope of proposed cook times.

- Cook time will likewise rely upon the thickness of your apple cuts. On the off chance that they are slender, they may cook somewhat faster.

- I propose not cutting them too slender, as they would then be able to consume without real crisping.

- completely firm when done; however, don't fuss. They will fresh after cooling.

- The apple chips crisper for nibbling, however gentler for garnish granola.

- For an alternate flavor profile, follow this recipe and use pears rather than apples.

One-Bowl Gluten-Free Chocolate Cake

This is a dazzling gluten-free chocolate cake that is ideal for all seasons.

Ingredients

- 3 huge eggs

- 1 cup (128g) almond flour

- 2/3 cup (85g) sugar

- 1/3 cup (78ml) overwhelming cream

- 1/4 cup (59ml) coconut oil dissolved

- 1/4 cup (32g) unsweetened cocoa powder

- 1 tsp baking powder

- ½ tsp orange get-up-and-go

- 1/8 cup (16g) hacked pecans

- 1/8 cup (16g) hacked walnuts

- unsalted spread at room temperature

Instructions

- Butter a 7-inch round baking dish and line the base with material paper.

- Place all ingredients into a huge bowl. With a hand blender on medium speed, beat until the hitter is light and soft. This is significant for keeping the cake from being excessively thick.

- Carefully overlap the nuts into the hitter to keep the air in.

- Pour cake player into the skillet and spread firmly with aluminum foil.

- Place in the air fryer bin and cook for 45 minutes at 325F.

- Remove the thwart and afterward cook for an extra 10-15 mins, until a blade embedded in the inside confesses all.

- Take work out of air fryer and set on a cooling rack for 10 mins. At that point, expel cake from the skillet and let it cool for an extra 20 mins.

- Slice and serve.

Tips

- It is essential to blend the ingredients until the hitter is pleasant and feathery. Generally, your cake will be excessively thick.

- Make sure to utilize oven gloves while expelling the cake container from the air fryer.

- I utilized a blend of pecans and walnuts, yet hacked almonds or hazelnuts are additionally incredible decisions.

Air Fryer and Campfire Nutella Smores

A delectable curve on the late spring exemplary that you can appreciate throughout the entire year!

Ingredients

- 4 graham wafers cut down the middle (or 8 bread rolls of your decision)

- 4 kind sized marshmallows on the off chance that extremely gigantic, at that point utilize 2 cut down the middle

- Strawberries and Raspberries

- 4 tsp of Nutella

Instructions

Air Fryer Smores:

- Preheat the air fryer to 350 F/180 C.

- Place 4 graham saltine parts (or 4 scones) in the air fryer container.

- Put 1 marshmallow over every graham wafer half.

- Cook for 5 mins, till marshmallow, is decent and brilliant.

- Add the berries and the Nutella.

- Top each with a graham saltine half (or roll).

- Serve and appreciate it!

Barbecue and Campfire Smores

- Toast the 4 marshmallows over open fire or barbecue till brilliant.

- Place 1 toasted marshmallow over a graham wafer half (or bread).

- Then layer on the berries and Nutella.

- Top with another graham saltine half (or roll).

Serve and appreciate it!

CHAPTER SIX

WEEKLY AIR FRYER MEAL PLAN

This Air Fryer Meal Plan incorporates an entire month of principle dishes in addition to 4 breakfasts, four sides, and even four air fryer treats. Track with as recorded, or don't hesitate to change it up and make your optimal meal plan. Prepare for the Air Fryer to take your meal planning to an unheard-of level.

- Main meals for 4 entire weeks

- 4 breakfasts

- 4 side dish/snacks

- 4 sweets

Why a Meal Plan?

As the idiom goes, 'neglecting to plan is planning to fall flat.' That is undoubtedly the situation in my home. Furthermore, that is the reason this Air Fryer meal plan is intended to make your life EASY.

When you attempt meal planning, you will never need to return. Need additionally persuading? Here are only a couple of ways you will profit by following this meal plan:

- Grocery shopping is increasingly proficient. Not anymore a minute ago excursions to the store for that night's meal.

- Saves you time. With a bit of planning, you take out each one of those everyday choices about what to make.

- Reduces squander by not purchasing additional ingredients at the general store 'if something goes wrong.'

- Gets the whole family required since they can help pick the weekly meal plan request. What's more, since they comprehend what's for dinner, they can even contribute and help in the kitchen.

- Trying new things is enjoyable. Planning out your meals ahead of time implies you can plan for some experimentation and have some good times making increasingly 'modern to you' dishes.

Meal planning is the best thing ever!

Air Fryer Meal Plan: Week 1 Mains

1. Air Fryer Whole Chicken

2. Air Fryer Cauliflower Curry

3. Classic Air Fryer Meatloaf

4. Air Fryer Chicken Fried Rice

5. Smoky Air Fryer Ribs

6. Shrimp Tempura Sushi Burrito

7. Apple, Cranberry and Sausage Stuffed Acorn Squash

Air Fryer Meal Plan: Week 2 Mains

1. Air Fryer Chicken Breast

2. Air Fryer Steak with Herb Lemon Butter

3. Air Fryer Chicken Quesadillas

4. Air Fryer Salmon

5. Crunchy Air Fryer Grilled Cheese

6. Air Fryer Chicken Shawarma Bowl

7. Madagascan Bean Stew

Air Fryer Meal Plan: Week 3 Mains

1. Air Fryer Chicken Thighs

2. Juicy Air Fryer Hamburgers

3. Crispy Air Fryer Chickpea Tacos

4. Air Fryer Crispy Golden Fish

5. Air Fryer Hot Dogs

6. Air Fryer Pork Chops

7. Air Fryer Stuffed Peppers

Air Fryer Meal Plan: Week 4 Mains

1. Crispy Air Fryer Chicken Wings with Parmesan

2. Cilantro Lime Air Fryer Shrimp Skewers

3. Air Fryer Turkey Meatballs

4. Air Fryer Pita Bread Pizza

5. Air Fryer Salmon Patties

6. Vegetarian Tacos

7. Beef Steak Kabobs

Air Fryer Meal Plan: Breakfasts

1. Air Fryer French Toast Sticks {Vegetarian}

2. Air Fryer Breakfast Frittata{Low Carb, Keto, Gluten Free}

3. Air Fryer Bacon{Keto, Low Carb, Paleo, Gluten Free}

4. Air Fryer Plantains{Vegan, Paleo, Gluten-Free, Whole 30}

Air Fryer Meal Plan: Sides and Snacks

1. Air Fryer Tater Tots {Vegan, Gluten Free}

2. Crispy Air Fryer Brussels Sprouts {Vegan, Keto, Low Carb, Paleo, Gluten-Free, Whole 30}

3. Air Fryer Sweet Potato Fries {Vegan, Keto, Paleo, Gluten-Free, Whole 30}

4. Air Fryer Buffalo Cauliflower Wings {Vegan, Keto, Paleo, Low Carb, Gluten Free}

Air Fryer Meal Plan: Desserts

1. 1 Bowl Gluten Free Chocolate Cake {Gluten Free}

2. Air Fryer Apple Chips {Vegan, Low Carb, Paleo, Whole 30, Gluten Free}

3. Air Fryer Blueberry Hand Pies {Vegetarian}

4. Healthier Air Fryer Donuts {Vegetarian}

The most effective method to Clean an Air Fryer

To assist you with thinking about your new most loved machine, we've assembled a snappy and straightforward cleaning guide beneath. Also, but if you need motivation to filthy it up (you know so that you can clean it), attempt one of these delicious air fryer recipes, from seared pickles to chicken wings.

What to Wash After every Use?

The bushel, plate, and container can be washed simply like you would some other dish: with cleanser and warm water. Or then again, if you don't want to remove them by hand (and we don't accuse you), place them in the dishwasher. Most air fryers have dishwasher-safe pieces. However, check the instruction manual for your particular model first, just no doubt. Dry the entirety of the parts totally before you reassemble the air fryer.

When the bushel or skillet has heated on oil, absorb it boiling water and cleanser for 20 to 30 minutes. At that point, evacuate the now-relaxed gunk with a scour brush. To clean the inside, expel the crate, plate, and skillet to clean within the air fryer. Just run a sodden fabric or wipe with a tad of dish cleanser over the whole inside and wipe it dry.

What to Wash Occasionally

Since there's almost no oil associated with air searing, there's additionally minimal oily buildup, so you don't have to clean the outside of the air fryer as often as possible. Utilize a clammy material to wipe down the outside of each couple of employments. Ensure you unplug it first! Additionally, check the curl. When there's oil or buildup on the warming curl, let the unplugged machine cool. At that point, wipe the loop with a soggy fabric— naturally like you would with the warming component on an electric stove.

Air Fryer Deep-Cleaning Tips

When you notice a foul smell originating from your air fryer, odds are there are food particles caught someplace in or on it. Combine baking pop and water to shape a glue. At that point, utilize a scour brush or an old toothbrush to completely clean the inside of the air fryer. (Truly, did you realize baking soft drink could do this?!)

Never utilize metal utensils to evacuate scraps or heated on oil from the fryer. It can harm the non-stick covering and keep your fryer from working appropriately. Realizing how to clean an air fryer isn't hard, yet it is essential to think about and broaden the life of your machine.

Air Fryer versus Oven: What's the Difference and Which Is Healthier?

An air fryer is a conservative, ledge machine that utilizations convection warming to course air around your food. The food is held inside in a container, and a fan quickly moves air around the food, encompassing it likewise to food submerged in hot oil in a profound fryer. At last, it functions admirably to give food that firm, seared surface without a great deal of extra fat. Air fryers utilize next to zero oil to get a similar impact as customary profound broiling.

How is air broiling not quite the same as baking in an oven?

Conventional ovens work by delivering heat from a component (either gas or electric). The warmth is gradually scattered through the oven after some time. On account of convection ovens, that time is accelerated by the utilization of a fan—like the one of every air fryer.

Also, air fryers utilize fast air innovation to make heat rather than a component. That encourages them to heat up substantially more rapidly than an oven (also that they're a whole lot littler, as well). That little size encourages them to circle the warmth all the more equally, crisping up your food without problem areas.

Which technique is more advantageous?

There genuine inquiry: Is the air fryer more beneficial than baking food in the oven? You don't have to utilize any oil whatsoever. That is because the unit warms up, so it's hot enough to fresh your food with no additional oil. I can't state that I've, at any point, had the option to accomplish that in an oven (even a convection oven).

This being stated, if almost no oil is being added to the dishes you're making in the air fryer, those dishes are similarly as sound as though you would have prepared them. The nutritional aren't changing, only the system, so air fry however much you might want!

If you have the cash to put resources into another machine and the space to store it, at that point, but it all on the line! The air fryer gives you the crunchy surface of singed foods without the additional oil and fat.

This Is What an Air Fryer Does to Your Food

The air fryer furor is clearing the country, yet what is an air fryer? Is it extremely worth your well-deserved money? This helpful apparatus professes to mirror the consequences of profound singing with simply tourists and a small measure of oil. The air fryer is an amped-up ledge convection oven. Its conservative space encourages considerably quicker cooking. The highest point of the unit holds a warming component and a fan. Sight-seeing rushes down and around food put in a fryer-style bushel. This fast flow makes the food fresh, much like profound broiling. Cleanup is excessively simple, as well, and most units have dishwasher-safe parts.

What would you be able to make in it?

Air fryers make a phenomenal showing concocting solidified foods that are intended to taste rotisserie—think solidified French fries, chicken wings, and mozzarella sticks. They additionally work superbly with comparative recipes produced using scratch. Perhaps the best part is that air fryers can prepare, as well.

What wouldn't you be able to make?

You can't make anything with a fluid hitter like this Crispy Beer Battered Fish (except if you freeze it first). You additionally can't make anything in huge amounts, so in case you're nourishing a family, be set up to cook in bunches.

Different interesting points...

- **Cost.** On the expensive side of home appliances, air fryers run somewhere in the range of $100 and $300, relying upon size and highlights. Locate the best air fryer for your way of life.

- **Space.** Greater than a toaster, the air fryer is anything but a little machine. You'll have to surrender important stockpiling (or counter) space to house one.

- **Skills.** Air fryers are fitting and play. Spot your food in the crate, set the time, and the temperature and bam! You're cooking.

- **Taste and surface.** With the help of an air fryer, will give you results a lot nearer to profound broiling than your oven will, toward the day's end, it's as yet not the equivalent.

- **Healthier?** The contention can be made that it produces more beneficial food by utilizing less oil. Solidified French fries arranged in the air fryer contain somewhere in the range of 4 and 6 grams of fat versus their southern-style partner at an astounding 17 grams for every serving.

Toward the day's end, this is an entirely smooth device. At the point when you're concocting things like French fries or chicken chunks, you can't beat it. The outcomes are superior to oven searing, and your kitchen remains cool. While it works admirably cooking different meats and vegetables, the air fryer truly sparkles at mock profound singing. So on the off chance that you don't typically eat southern-style foods, it's most likely not worth the venture.

Lightning Source UK Ltd.
Milton Keynes UK
UKHW021838010221
378084UK00003B/563